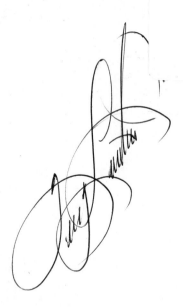

Commencement Messages

Education Starts,
Not Ends,
With the Diploma

Dr. Wright L. Lassiter, Jr.
Chancellor
Dallas County Community College District
Dallas, Texas

Order this book online at www.trafford.com
or email orders@trafford.com

Most Trafford titles are also available at major online book retailers.

Printed in the United States of America.

ISBN: 978-1-4269-9578-1 (sc)
ISBN: 978-1-4269-9579-8 (hc)
ISBN: 978-1-4269-9580-4 (e)

Library of Congress Control Number: 2011917028

Trafford rev. 09/21/2011

 www.trafford.com

North America & international
toll-free: 1 888 232 4444 (USA & Canada)
phone: 250 383 6864 ♦ fax: 812 355 4082

Contents

Part Two
Education Starts, Not Ends With The Diploma
Selected Quotations

Part Three
End Notes

Acknowledgments

Each time I am privileged to cause my thoughts and spoken words to be placed in print, grateful appreciation is extended to my wife, Bessie, for her constant support and encouragement. She encourages me during our quiet moments together by saying that others could benefit from the gifts that the Lord has blessed me with.

Through her love and support for fifty-three years, my pen has produced ten published works.

For this book I have been encouraged, assisted and supported to an unusual degree by Toni Barajas. She walked with me through the arduous task of formatting, editing, proof-reading, and the constant back and forth with the publishing team. I am deeply indebted to her for the attention to detail that is required for high-quality published works. This work would not have been produced had she not been there to provide a comforting word during difficult times.

Finally, I acknowledge the support received from Eddie Walker who designed the cover for this book and all of the other published works through the Trafford Publishing Group.

Introduction

My beloved mother introduced me to the magic and mystery of words when she taught me to read at age 3. She told me that I advanced so rapidly that she elected to enroll me in a "private school" that was operated by a wonderful little lady named Mrs. Chavis. This little school was a large room in her home, but I learned so much under Mrs. Chavis that she remained a dear friend until her departure for heaven many years later.

My fascination with words deepened when my father would bring discarded magazines and books home from residences where he was performing construction work. On one such occasion my father brought home not only magazines and books, but also a discarded 1923 Underwood typewriter. With my now having reading material and a "machine," I developed a "hunt and peck" style and began to not only read, but also write.

Needing an elective in high school, I enrolled in a typing class. I could now transfer my "hunt and peck" style, into the informed use of more up-to-date typewriters. Being the only male in the class, I had the immediate challenge of not being left behind by my female classmates. To everyone's surprise, I moved to the head of the class by typing just fewer than 100 words per minute at the end of the first semester.

With my newly acquired skills, and some meager funds, I began casting about for an upgraded typewriter. When my father and I went to the office supply store to purchase a used typewriter, he surprised me by electing to purchase a brand new Smith Corona portable typewriter. Now I had everything that I needed to continue my odyssey with words and the printed page.

As a part of my college curriculum, a course in public speaking was required. My instructor, Mrs. Elihue Barden, had a unique teaching strategy for persons with rapid speech patterns (as I did). That was to cause students to learn to speak with two marbles in our mouths (and avoid swallowing the marbles). Once again, I moved to the head of the class and continued my odyssey with words through a variety of public presentations.

The odyssey with words continued when I participated in two other programs during my life and career at Tuskegee Institute in Alabama. Those were the Evelyn Wood Speed Reading course, and Toastmasters International. Both programs served as valuable adjuncts and tools in my continuing odyssey—yea love affair—with words and the spoken word.

My career as an educator, public servant, and minister has required me to continually use words. I recall reading a short passage by Reverend Henry Ward Beecher in <u>Proverbs from Plymouth Pulpit</u> *(1887) that has continually fascinated me: "All words are pegs to hang ideas on."*

Two contemporary writers also had cogent expressions regarding words. Leo Rosten's (1972) thoughts are: "Words—they sing, they hurt, they teach, they sanctify. They were man's first immeasurable feat of magic. They liberated us from ignorance and our barbarous past. For without these marvelous scribbles, which build letters into words, words into sentences, sentences into systems and sciences and creeds, man would be forever confined to the self-isolated prison of the cuttlefish or the chimpanzee. 'One picture is worth ten thousand words,' goes the timeworn Chinese maxim. 'But,' one writer tartly said, 'It takes words to say that.' We live by words: love, truth, God. We fight for words: freedom, country, fame. We die for words: liberty, glory, honor. They bestow the priceless gift of articulacy on our minds and hearts—from 'Mama' to 'infinity.' And the men who truly shape our destiny, the giants who teach us, inspire us, lead us to deeds of immortality, are those who use words with clarity, grandeur, and passion!"

Garry Willis, Professor of American Culture and Public Policy at Northwestern University, had equally cogent expressions, which impressed me. He writes, "Words are the instruments with which we build our world—our bridges to each other. I cannot see your thoughts directly. You must convey them to me, clumsily or well."

In this limited selection of speeches and presentations I have diligently sought to convey my thoughts through the spoken and written word. My hope is that other readers will find utility in my use of words.

Wright L. Lassiter, Jr.

The Perspective for Commencement

During my long career in higher education I have been privileged to address many graduating classes. These addresses have spanned from high schools to community colleges, four-year colleges and universities. My consistent message is that education starts, and not ends, with the diploma. The second consistent theme is that one must always have goals in life.

The introduction to this collection of messages is a short commencement address on the importance of goals.

Always Have Goals in Your Life

Congratulations on this important achievement in your life! You must view this achievement as one of the most significant achievements in your educational and life journey. File this thought in your consciousness for consistent reference: Education starts, and not ends, with the diploma. You have arrived at this point because you did set a goal in life. This process must continue on a daily basis. When you do that, it enables you to see whether you are on track to achieving them, or whether you need to make some adjustments.

It's like a navigator of a great ship setting off on an ocean voyage. The navigator will lay out the track on a large chart, showing all the points along the path that the ship is to travel. The track will be frequently updated by navigational fixes, showing where the ship actually is in relation to the desired track. If winds and current have pushed the ship off course, you must steer certain degrees to the right or left in order to get back on course. It's the same in life, where we have to adjust our actions in order to get back on track and realize our goals.

Goals will add focus to your life. They will create activity and generate the kind of excitement you need to realize your full potential. Goals enable you to build a solid foundation under your dreams.

In setting your goals always think positively about yourself and your ability. If you don't practice this no can do it for you. Even more important, if you follow this practice you will find that in most cases people will take you as you see yourself. If you see yourself as confident and competent, then that is the way most people are going to see and treat you.

Always strive to be disciplined and always strive for excellence without excuses. Set high goals for yourself, for everything thing starts with you.

Finally, set goals for yourself that are higher than those goals anyone else sets for you. You will never regret it. Remember that in life you must function both as an individual and as members of organizations. Dr. Martin Luther King, Jr. recognized the value of teamwork. When accepting the Nobel Peace Prize in 1964 he said: "Every time I take a flight, I am always mindful of the many people who make a successful journey possible—the known pilots and the unknown ground crew." The Nobel Peace Prize, he said, was being given to one of the pilots, but he was accepting it on behalf of the crew. That is a powerful lesson at commencement!

One of the consistent themes in my commencement addresses is that you must accept a larger share of the responsibility for your lives. There are many things "out there" that could be labeled as obstacles. Never let them slow you down. Overcome them and never give in.

My development period as an administrator and educator was spent at that venerable institution founded by Booker T. Washington—Tuskegee Institute. At Moton Field in Tuskegee those courageous pilots that came to be known as the Tuskegee Airmen, attained their training by focusing on six points that they took with them through training and then into combat in World War II.

> *Aim High*
> *Believe in Yourself*
> *Use Your Brain*
> *Be Ready to Go*
> *Never Quit*
> *Expect to Win*

There is no royal road in charting your career and life, and there is no easy path to success. Hopefully, if you practice some of the strategies that you will find in this message, you will discern useful tools for your personal tool box.

Congratulations and remember that education starts, not ends, with the diploma. I close with some words from a YMCA chief executive officer that I embrace and I commend them to you:

> *Watch*

> *Watch your thoughts; they become words.*
> *Watch your words; they become actions.*
> *Watch your actions; they become habits.*
> *Watch your habits; they become character.*
> *Watch your character; it becomes your destiny.*

PART ONE

COMMENCEMENT & RELATED MESSAGES

The University of North Texas
Denton, Texas

THE HERITAGE OF TRUTH:

EDUCATION AND HUMANE VALUES

It is a great pleasure and privilege to be on the campus of the University of North Texas once again. As the largest comprehensive university in north Texas, this university has developed an honored reputation since it's founding in 1890. Today this is one of the state's most dynamic and forward-looking institutions. You have an earned reputation at the regional and national levels in a number of important programs and disciplines.

This convocation represents an occasion when we can visit with subject of values, personal and cultural.

Education and Values

What are values, exactly? In the abstract, values are the internal feelings we have about what are good, bad, indifferent—useful or superfluous, beautiful or unattractive. In general, values are held by individuals, but on the basis of principles common to a group. Your family, your community, your country, culture or civilization. Values are the social codes that regulate our lives.

In colleges and universities, as well as in education generally, values are an issue of virtually constant concern. On the one hand there are those who claim that values are subjective, individual, and irrelevant to the business of conveying factual knowledge. From this vantage, values have no place in education. In the first place, to attempt to teach or study them infringes on the rights of those who hold particular sets of values, as well as on the rights of those who reject them.

In the second place, subjective values can bias or prejudice the outcome of scholarly inquiry and research, which are supposed to be value-free.

Now on the other hand there are those who believe that it is impossible to exclude values from education, and far from being excluded, they should be required. Some representatives of this school of thought even go so far as to claim that higher education should stand or fall according to its capacity for dealing with values. As Charles Muscatine writes in The Future of University Education as an Idea: "Either the university of the future will take hold of the connections between knowledge and human values, or it will sink quietly into the noncommittal moral stupor of the rest of the knowledge industry."

I suppose there may well be an intermediate position, in this instance based on the question of priorities. As a character in a Brecht play might put it—"First grub—then values."

Democracy and Public Education

Well, as I have said, these are not new issues. I should like to suggest, however, that they have become far more critical with the advent of democratic society, with its dependence on public higher education for mass audiences.

The reason for this is simple. When education was something restricted largely to a ruling elite, it had to deal only with the consensual values of a relatively small, culturally, homogenous group. Students were very largely male, young, white, sound of body, affluent, and already well schooled—not only academically, but in the social graces as well. Thus in universities such as Cambridge in the late 1800s, for example, it was very easy to know what values an education should include. They were the clear-cut, traditionally defined values of an English gentleman.

But if we look back from across the Atlantic, we find that, even in the late 1800s, the constituency for American higher education had already grown much more diverse. The Morrill Land-Grant Act of 1862 had expanded both the audience and the goals of United States colleges and universities. Students were no longer just members of the well-to-do upper crust, pursuing degrees that would prepare them for careers in the professions and life in polite society. They were also the sons and daughters of farmers, merchants, laborers, artisans, and others. They were the burgeoning middle and working classes of the new nation.

They were studying for a far greater range of reasons, and pursuing a far greater range of goals. Not least, I should add, they subscribed to a far greater range of values, and those values played important roles in their educational careers. They were concerned not with participation in a traditional elite society, but rather with building a new, broad-based, and ever changing society. They honored not the inherited virtues of being well born, but the earned virtues of energy, hard work, and accomplishment. They believed, in sum, in the eminently radical, eminently practical ideals of democracy and egalitarianism and the right to make a new way.

Following the Morrill Act's historic opening up of higher education, the constituency of United States colleges and universities experienced an ongoing diversification that has extended down to the present. The GI Bill, the development of junior and community colleges, equal opportunity and affirmative action, open-door and full-opportunity programs; all of these brought into the student population not only large numbers of students, but vastly different kinds of students. As pluralistic as were their backgrounds, so to were their values and value systems.

Because of the American commitment to an educated citizenry, this pluralism of students and values has become an integral feature of U.S. higher education, particularly, I may say, public higher education. Yet because there are so many values with which we must deal, we also find that the potential for conflict among values has increased. That is why I said earlier that a democratic society poses the old question of values in education with a new and especially compelling urgency.

Procedural Values

In a democracy, then, the fact is that competing and even conflicting values somehow manage to coexist. Sometimes in harmony, sometimes not, but without engaging in all out war. How is this so?

It is so because democracies have two kinds of values. The first kind is the familiar specific values of many cultural heritages and varieties of personal experience. I, for example, may say that service to the community is the highest goal. You, on the other hand, might argue that self-realization is the only acceptable measure of man. I may believe in economic competition and the free market. You might argue passionately for a regulated economy and social responsibility. Nevertheless, we can live next door to each other, get along with each other, and even become fast friends.

We can do these things because although we disagree on certain substantive values, we share what I call the procedural values of democracy. Specific values have to do with ends; procedural have to do with how we achieve our ends.

Generally speaking, it seems to me that the values most central in education, particularly in public higher education, are procedural values. They are the values that have to do not so much with what we are going to do, as with how we are going to go about it. To decide and resolve the differences and to arrive at consensus when a single value must dominate. They are the values that allow us our differences of opinion, our differences of direction and interest, and also allow us the peace and freedom to pursue them.

Generosity, Modesty, and Truth

What are the procedural values of democracy that are most central to the purposes of education? Let me briefly discuss three—generosity, modesty and truth.

The most obvious and perhaps the most fundamental procedural value for democratic education is generosity. Perhaps you thought I was going to say tolerance. For tolerance is what makes possible the coexistence of opposed views, either between individuals in a classroom, or within an institution of learning and scholarship. I say generosity rather than tolerance in order to stress a difference of spirit.

Tolerance accepts difference, divergence, and diversity. Generosity encourages it, listens to it, engages in dialogue with it, and grows by experiencing it. Generosity considers the pluralism of public education to be a strength, not merely an unavoidable inconvenience. It was this generosity that Ralph Waldo Emerson had in mind, I believe, when he wrote that ". . . before all other considerations . . . I think it is the main guard to a correct judgment, I may say the bulwark of all that is sacred to man . . . now to accept degrading views."

A second procedural value central to both democracy and education is modesty. There are questions to which education and scholarly inquiry can offer specific and viable answers, and there are other questions whose answers will be forever elusive. We may be able to find ways to replace fossil fuels as the energy basis of our economy, but we will never be able to give a final resolution of the problem— what is humanity?

To accept change, to be aware of the limits of inquiry, is the essence of learning in an open society; to demand answers that will hold well forever, universally and absolutely, is the first step toward the philosophy of totalitarianism. As Reinhold Niebuhr says, "God give us the serenity to accept what cannot be changed, courage to change what should be changed, and wisdom to distinguish the one from the other."

And now let me apparently contradict myself by saying that the last value that education must foster is a love of truth. Truth, that is, as something that does not change, in its essence, and something that is in a fundamental sense universal. If a democratic education shies away universals and absolutes, how then can I call for an allegiance to this rather metaphysical idea of truth?

I do so by saying that democracy pursues truth without ever claiming or hoping to claim to have ultimately captured it at any point in time. Throughout history, people have asked many questions in many ways, and they have received many answers. The diversity of their researches has been wonderful. Yet beneath the surface flux, we can discern, though we can perhaps not express, something fundamental, something ineluctably basic, combining the manifold philosophical values of reality, beauty, and justice into a single face of truth. It is humankind's heritage always to seek to look upon this face of truth, but never to delude ourselves that we see, or shall see it clearly and in full.

In the final analysis, these procedural values of generosity, modesty, and the love of truth transcend all the more limited values that contend in the arenas of democracy and higher education alike. These are the values that I submit we all should endeavor to internalize. Now your questions.

HONORING YESTERDAY:

CHALLENGING TOMORROW

No One Told Us It Was Going to Be Easy

This famous quote of Frederick Douglas written in 1849 is instructive in that it still speaks about the hardships inherent in reform and the claims of human liberty.

"The whole history of the progress of human liberty shows that all concessions yet made to her august claims, have been born of earnest struggle. The conflict has been exciting, agitating, all-absorbing and for the time being, putting all other tumults to silence, it must do this or it does nothing. If there is no struggle, there is no progress. Those who profess to favor freedom and yet deprecate agitation, are men who want crops without plowing up the ground, they want rain without thunder and lighting. They want the ocean without the awful roar of its many waters."

This struggle may be a moral one; or it may be a physical one; but it must be a struggle. Power concedes nothing without a demand. It never did and it never will. Find out just what people will submit to, and you have found out what the amount of injustice and wrong, which will be imposed upon them; and these, will continue until they are resisted with either words or blows, or with both.

The limits of tyrants are prescribed by the endurance of those whom they oppress. Men may not get all they pay for in the world; but they most certainly pay for all they get. If we ever get free from all of the oppression and wrongs heaped upon us, we must pay for their removal. We must do this by labor, by suffering, by sacrifice, and, if need be by our lives and lives of others.

Continuing with the quotes from Douglas, he said, "No one told us it was going to be easy." He continued:

> *"If there is no struggle, there is no progress.*
> *There is no love,*
> *No yearning for peace,*
> *No trials for justice,*
> *No struggle for unity,*
> *No fight for freedom without a road*
> *To block the way of life and love;*

But I can assure you there is no resistance, be it military, political, social, or economical that can stand forever against freedom. We as blacks and minorities have to get into politics, so that it will be politics for the people and not politics for the politicians. Politics must be transformed into programs and procedures of justice and sanity and not the continuation of the old power politics of madness and meanness. We have to get into the economy to make it serve humanity and not just enrich per cent of the people of the earth at the expense of the 80 percent who lack the basic necessities for bare subsistence.

We have to break into the worlds of industry, high technology, and business to ensure that money will be used to help people rather than to destroy them in the name of profit. We have to get into the struggle for unity and freedom so that all people in the world may share fully in the bounty and beauty of the earth.

We have to continue to speak out, walk out, and talk out against injustice and the denial of rights to oppressed peoples. We must not forget the memorable words of Dr. Martin Luther King, Jr., "we must fight the struggle until justice rolls down as waters and righteousness as mighty stream." If musicians can raise $70 million with one concert and another $50 million with one record that addressed the moral outrage of starving millions ("We Are One, We Are the World"), then collectively there is no limit to what we can accomplish!!

There are those in America who still want to contain the black race behind walls and stifle the fulfillment of their potential. They will say that because you are black you are inferior, you are untouchable, uneducable; that you are to be defined, contained, restricted.

They will say that you cannot participate as a full partner in the world economy, that you cannot live where you please, but must be content to dwell in the redlined ghetto.

Also, they will say that you cannot strive for excellence in science and math, but only in sports and entertainment—but we must say No Way!

We must say, This is our country and we demand our share of the money, the land, the knowledge, the freedom, the power, the leadership and everything else that is good, right and just!

But the way to these God-given blessings is not easy. There are many that still stand there blocking the way, but "No one said it would be easy!"

The late Justice Thurgood Marshall in one of the most eloquent statements about our struggle, in the Bakke case, said the following:

"The position of the Negro today in America is the tragic but inevitable
consequence of centuries of unequal treatment. Measured by any bench-
mark of comfort or achievement, meaningful equality remains a distant
dream for the Negro."

It is more than a little ironic that, after several hundred years of class-based discrimination against Negroes, the court is unwilling to hold that a class-based remedy for that discrimination is permissible, in declining to so hold, today's judgment ignores the fact that for several hundred years African Americans have been discriminated against, not as individuals, but rather solely because of the color of their skin. It is unnecessary as we come to the end of the 20th century to have individual African Americans demonstrate that they have been victims of racial discrimination. The racism of our society has been so pervasive that none, regardless of wealth or position, has managed to escape its impact.

The experience of African Americans is America . . . is not merely the history of slavery alone but also that a whole people who were marked inferior by the law, and that mark has endured. The dream of America as the great melting pot has not been realized by the African American (in spite of all the progress that individuals have made); for many they have not even made it into the pot!

Those who say that things have reached a point in America that we should adopt a color-blind philosophy and concept should be reminded of what Justice Blackmun said in the Bakke case:

"I yield to no one in my earnest hope that the time will come when an 'Affirmative

Action program' is unnecessary and is, in truth, only a relic of the past."

Justice Blackmun stated further:

> *"In order to look beyond race, we must first take account of race. There is no other*
> *way and, in order to treat some persons equally, we must treat them differently. We*
> *zcannot—we dare not—let the equal protection clause perpetuate racial supremacy."*

To be one-half slave and one-half free it still to be a slave. Do you know of any black man or woman in America who is totally and completely free? All of us who have black skin are still regarded and treated differently—just because of our skin color.

My friends, I submit to you that there are people in America, who in devious ways only known to themselves, who say that African Americans should be pulling themselves up by their own bootstraps and that race is not a factor in the upward mobility of African Americans in America today.

This may not sound good, but we must admit that we still live in a racist society where the presumption of race alone has been used to determine how far we can go and how high we can rise.

We have been enslaved,
Segregated,
Rejected,
Excluded,
Mistreated,
Locked out,
Exploited,
Despised

Disenfranchised, and
Discouraged.

Why? For one reason only, and that is the fact that we have black skin. To proffer color blindness as a solution to our suffering takes an obtuse, cruel and ironic twist of mind.

As we look at the situation that confronts us as a people, we must acknowledge that we have enough courage to proceed. We have enough optimism to refresh, resurrect, and give true meaning to those four words etched in marble at the U.S. Supreme Court Building in Washington, D.C.: "Equal justice under law."

We have enough love to cast out fear; we have enough faith to press through darkness. Rosa Parks refused to go to the back of the bus in Montgomery, Alabama in December 1955, and changed the whole Civil Rights movement in the South. What made her keep walking, when her feet were tired, even though she had no answer! What made her go on in spite of her life being threatened? She had no human help. She had no tangible solution to the problem. Only her dignity and the fact that she had had enough. She continued on her journey. Can we do like Rosa Parks did? Can we live on, love on, struggle on, trusting where we cannot trace, hoping where we cannot see, believing when we cannot understand? What did Douglas say, "no one said it would be easy."

We still have obstacles to overcome. We cannot cancel the journey, stop walking, resign from the struggle, give up the fight, throw in the towel, or surrender to injustice, intolerance and racism.

Let me say that as we all know, there is always a struggle, between Faith and Doubt. Follow me on this little <u>faith and doubt journey</u>.

FAITH always speaking inspiration and encouragement and DOUBT always speaking discouragement and despair.

FAITH tells us that all things are possible. While DOUBT says we can accomplish nothing.

FAITH says that through the constitution of the United States and the Declaration of Independence, victory will be ours, but DOUBT says we are defeated before we start.

DOUBT has never achieved anything:

> *It has never planted a tree,*
> *Never written a book,*
> *Never comforted the weary,*
> *Never healed the sick,*
> *Never reared a child,*
> *Never educated a student,*
> *Never solved a problem,*
> *Never won a case and never enjoyed victory!*

But by FAITH we are able to accomplish all that we do.

It is by faith that the Urban League has been in existence and is still fighting, kicking and very much alive after 88 years of struggle.

It is by FAITH that the surgeon picks up the scalpel,
By FAITH the engineer builds a bridge;
By FAITHJ that the pilot flies the aircraft;
By FAITH the farmer sows his crops;
By FAITH the unskilled receives training;
By FAITH the unemployed find jobs.

It is by FAITH that when black children begin each day of the school year uttering these powerful words "I pledge allegiance to the flag of the United States of America and to the republic for which it stands, one nation under God, indivisible, with liberty and justice for all," they know full-well that liberty and justice for all its citizens is not fully a reality.

It is by FAITH that Booker T. Washington created Tuskegee Institute from nothing.

By FAITH that W.E.B. DuBois created the NAACP.

By FAITH that Jesse Owens lectured to Adolf Hitler with his feet.

By FAITH that the late Justice Thurgood Marshall sat on the U.S. Supreme Court as the first African American citizen.

By FAITH that Martin Luther King, Jr. declared a deathless dream.

By FAITH that Dr. Charles Drew discovered blood plasma.

By FAITH that Jackie Robinson broke the barrier of segregation in organized baseball and withstood all of the evil actions of his fellow players.

By FAITH that the late Coleman A. Young resurrected the city of Detroit when people said that it was dead!

By FAITH that Oprah Winfrey and Bill Cosby enjoy supreme ratings for their television programs.

By FAITH John Johnson, publisher and editor of Ebony and Jet magazines said, "I will bring to America the victories, struggles and heartaches of black people not told by anyone else."

The struggle must continue, so by FAITH we can do great things. We should never give up! By FAITH our children can enjoy all of the beauty and opportunities of their country and when they sing "My country 'tis of thee, sweet land of liberty" they will know that it has a true meaning.

It is by FAITH we will be free and we shall overcome. But "No one told us it was going to be easy." We have to work on, walk on, pray on, with FAITH in our hearts. For the power of FAITH that has sustained us has endured for generations. For the hand that moves us is the hand that rules the world. FAITH is the victory that overcomes the world.

As Frederick Douglas said: "If there is no struggle, there is no progress"; and, with struggle, with optimism and with FAITH, we shall indeed overcome!!

LEARNING:

THE WAY TO CONTROL YOUR FUTURE

The Proper Path to a Successful Career

It is always a great honor to address any group. I consider it a special privilege to address audiences of young men and women. I think everyone has the dream of one day being looked on as a role model by young people. We think that once we've made it in life, it's time to pass on our sage words of wisdom, to share our interesting experiences and valuable insights with those who are just starting out.

I believe it was George Bernard Shaw who said "youth is wasted on the young." And I am sure you've had plenty of older people, including your parents, give you lots of free advice on how to live, what to value and what to avoid, and how to manage your career.

Perhaps we could modify the words of Shaw thus: "adulthood is wasted on the middle aged." If you can preserve the way that you lead your life today into your later years, you are going to be way ahead of a lot of so-called "mature adults."

By this I do not mean that you should live in the same house as your parents for the rest of your life. Nor do I think you should keep up the level of food and drink you are consuming today.

Well, you ask, what is it that a student does—and that many adults stop doing too soon? Quite simply it's learning.

The willingness and an ability to learn is the key to your future success. It is not necessary that you go to the "right" university, or get the "right" job when you finish, or that you stay with one employer—or even one profession—for your entire working career. The important thing is to keep learning.

Please recall a practice from your school experiences. You are all used to changing your subject matter every time a bell rings. From what I remember about a school, that's a really unnatural and irritating way for a human being to live. But I also think it's a good analogy for what it will take for you to be successful in the new millennium.

An explanation is in order. Ten years ago, even five years ago, the North American workplace was a pretty stable place. There was a sort of social contract between workers and their employers that said: "if you give us your life, we will give you a successful career."

You may have heard the expression "climbing the ladder of success." Every big company had a career path that loyal, hardworking employees would follow. If you put in five years in this job, and ten years in that job, and three years in another job, you would eventually become a general manager, or a director, or a vice president, or even a president.

There were fast tracks and slower tracks. If you were willing to move a lot, or get posted to strange places, your career would move faster and you would climb higher up the ladder.

It was a dependable system. You would get a small raise every year, whether you deserved it or not. Your sons and daughters would possibly have summer jobs. And you would retire with a gold watch and a good pension.

Well, as you know, times have changed. During the 1980s there was this thing that happened called "massive restructuring," also known as "layoffs." A lot of companies in this country were forced to make major changes to their businesses in order to survive.

Global competition was one thing that drove these changes. Our industries couldn't just make widgets any more. We had to make them as cheaply, and have as high a quality, as Japan, or Germany, or Mexico, and so on.

Technology also drove those changes. If you didn't embrace new technology, your high-tech competitors would sweep you into the dustbin of history, or, they would simply delete you. Oil prices and monetary changes throughout the world also were an influence, along with educational advances.

My position is that all the change you have seen is going to be good for your careers. You see, the proverbial "social contract" has been broken. There is no more ladder of success as it was traditionally known.

In the old days, companies would look after their employees, and their employees would return the favor with undying loyalty. Today's reality is that you have to look out for yourself. To those who got kicked out of the old system, this is the scariest thing that ever happened. But to you, who are just starting out, it's a golden opportunity. More than any other time in the history of the modern workplace, you are in a position to call the shots when it comes to your career.

And that's where the learning skill that you already have, being able to change at the "ring of the bell," comes into play. Because the way to manage your career into the next century is to know how to get yourself from one learning opportunity to the next. And that could mean switching jobs as often as every six months. Switching companies as much as every two years. And completing switching disciplines or professions several times in your life.

I know this because I have lived it, and I continue to live it. I like to think that adulthood has not been wasted on me. I suppose you could say that even at my age, I still haven't grown up.

As you listen to me give you a brief history of my career, one thing will become evident. I have enjoyed every moment of it. What does a short history of my career mean to you? Well, what I discovered as I changed jobs, and careers over the years, is that each time I changed, I was able to add to my skills and knowledge.

The bell rang and I moved on to learn about the next thing. Sometimes I rang the bell myself. Here are some of the other lessons that I have learned. I have learned the importance of craft, and efficiency, and good work habits. I have learned what business is really about. I have learned what it's like to live inside a big, sometimes ugly, bureaucracy. Also how it can bore you to death, or crush you like a bug.

I have also learned I didn't have to be bored to death or crushed, and that I could make a difference. I have learned that people with lots of different kinds of experiences are highly valued. Every time that I have changed jobs I learned some more, and I add another arrow to my quiver.

One of the leading trend-watchers in this country is Marilyn Moats Kennedy. Her company advises big employers on trends in the workplace, and she writes and talks about office politics, and how to manage your career. She speaks and writes about the growing shortage of skilled, educated people in the workplace. As the baby boomers move on and begin to retire, there are not enough people for the new jobs that are being created in this booming economy. She says that for the first time in a long time, companies are having to compete for good people. This fits in perfectly with what I have been saying today; you are in a position of unprecedented power as you move ahead with your career. Because the more you know, and the more diverse your experience, the more in demand you will be.

The key is to constantly be looking for opportunities to change and learn. And that might mean within the organization that you're working for. It could mean changing organizations. And it could mean deciding, after picking up enough skills and experiences in the corporate world, to junk it all and work for yourself. But whatever you do, do it on your own terms, not someone else's. In fact, the more you take your career into your own hands, the more you will be rewarded with new opportunities to learn and to grow.

If there's one thing I want to leave with you today, it's that to have a successful career you always need to be looking at least one or two steps into the future. What you're doing today does not necessarily lead directly to where you want to be three, or five, or ten years from now.

But if you think in terms of what you need to learn next, instead of what job you think you need to have next, you will be a lot further ahead. Be constantly imagining paths for yourself. My advice is to always try to have at least three long-term paths when you imagine your future. You need to be constantly thinking about how you are going to get the skills and experience you need to get on to the next step.

On this journey of learning and discovery, if you ever arrive, that's when you are in trouble. The trip should never really end. Take my advice and carefully consider it. Keep learning. When that bell rings, be willing to change your job, your career, or whatever, in order to get satisfaction out of your working life.

A CHALLENGE TO THE BEST:

YOU HAVE TO BURN THE MIDNIGHT OIL

Tradition and protocol dictate that all speakers begin by telling how very happy and honored they are to before you. So I begin by telling you that I am humbled and honored to have the special privilege to address this audience today.

One of the reasons that I am glad to be here is that I know that you are the cream of the crop. You are the best and the brightest. You are the diamonds in the rough, making your way up the rough side of the mountain.

And for many of you, your very presence here today is a victory. For some of you are here not because of, but in spite of. The statisticians and the odds makers, the magazine writers and the newspaper journalists had written many of you off. They said you'd never make it this far. They said that you could lift and load, push and pull, punt and kick. They said that you could sing and dance, but that you could never invent and construct— scrutinize and analyze—develop and devise.

But here you are. You are those would not be denied. You beat the statistics, outperformed the predictors, outlasted your critics and disproved the doubters. And now you find yourself studying and mastering industrial robotics, regression analysis, network design, and the molecular composition of materials. You are calculating the age and origins of the universe. When you finish your studies here and move to advanced programs, you may help in developing cures for cancer and for being on teams that will design new scientific advances.

So ladies and gentlemen, you have come a long way, but one of the reasons I'm here today is to tell you that you cannot rest on your laurels now. I'm here to challenge you to be the best!

After all, grandma and granddaddy, Uncle Willie and Miss Bessie and all of the gang from the old neighborhood are expecting even greater things out of you. You have come a long way, but it does not yet appear what you are capable of becoming.

And you know as well as I do that in science, mathematics, engineering and technology, you have chosen fields that are not for the faint of heart. In these programs of study you have a great challenge before you. And you need to understand that in order to rise to this challenge, you are going to have to work! You are going to have to work harder than you've ever worked before. You're going to have to burn the midnight oil. That is, you're going to have to remember the words of the poet Longfellow: "The heights of great men reached and kept were not attained by sudden flight, but they, while their companions slept, were toiling upwards through the night."

You must realize that long nights and dogged determination are the unavoidable price of being that best that you can be. For you already possess the necessary tools to get the job done. And you would not have chosen science, mathematics, engineering and technology if you did not believe that you have what it takes to make it.

Yes, ladies and gentlemen, you've chosen the long road. But, on this road, you will have to remind yourselves over and over that there are no shortcuts and no magic keys to success. Someone once asked James Lofton, one of the best wide receivers to ever play in the NFL, "what are your tricks to the success that you have enjoyed on the gridiron?" Lofton replied, "I have five, let me share them with you. My first trick is to work harder than the other guy. My second trick is to always hustle. My third trick is to study and know what I'm doing when it's game time. My fourth trick is to always be prepared. The fifth and final trick is to never, never, never give up and never give in to mediocrity."

He was really articulating a strong message. What Lofton was really saying is that there are no tricks and there are no magic keys to success. Only hard work, sacrifice and a commitment to be the best at whatever you're going to do will get you there.

So whatever you have set your sights on, I encourage you to make your necessary investment. Make such an investment of time and energy, sweat and tears, sacrifice and struggle that you can be like a certain baseball player that I have heard described. This person said, "You can never be a real ball player until you have the heart, the confidence, and the chutzpah in the bottom of the ninth with the bases loaded, two outs and their best hitter at the plate to say—God, I hope he hits it to me."

You need to be just that sure of your preparation. And the world of work is no exception. Your college has placed you in the game. Now, you need to have the assurance that when you leave here, that with your academic training that you willing and ready to take on that so-called make or break project. And you don't become that cocky, that sure of yourself, that certain of your abilities, by taking any short cuts.

I once read of Michelangelo's reaction after being called a genius, a master of his craft. The great artist is said to have replied, simply but poignantly, "if they knew how much I put into my mastery, they wouldn't find it marvelous at all." And the same is true of anyone who is intent on being the best at what he or she does. For when they say that Michael Jordan is the best basketball player of all time, no one sees Jordan shoot the 487th free throw at 1 a.m. in the morning.

Likewise, no one is with Evander Holyfield when he runs that 17th mile at 5 a.m. in the morning. No one will be with you at 2 a.m. in the morning when you are running the 37th iteration of the program that is due to your professor at 8 a.m. the next morning. All that the rest of the world will know is that Michael Jordan scored 55 points last night. That Evander Holyfield defied the odds to become heavyweight champion of the world and somehow, when everyone else called it quits, threw up their hands and went to bed, somehow, you got that program to run. And, ladies and gentlemen, that's the type of dedication, that's the type of commitment that being the best requires.

You are all achievers, but everyone wasn't #1 in your high school class. Everyone cannot be #1 in this class when you reach the point of graduating. Nothing personal, just the facts of life. But, nevertheless, you've get to set, as your unwavering goal, to be the best that you can be. Whatever your area of study, there is no room for mediocrity. You cannot be comfortable with merely completing the prescribed course of study. Strive to be the best!

The story is told of an army general who went to lunch one day and ordered his favorite dish of broiled lobster. A lobster was brought to him minus a claw. The general immediately summoned the waiter to his table to complain. When the waiter arrived, he said—"General, sir, let me explain. This is a broiled lobster just like you ordered, but what you must understand is that lobsters are kept in a holding tank alive. While they're in the tank they often fight and sometimes lose a claw." To this, the general thundered back, "Then, for God's sake, bring me a winner!"
And that's your challenge ladies and gentlemen. It's not good enough to leave this university with just a degree. The world

today is looking for winners. Make sure you leave ready to convince the world that you are superbly trained and thoroughly able to compete against any student, from any university, in any city in the world. That's what your alma mater expects of you.

And that's what your parents expect of you. You see, it's one thing to be denied, as many of our parents and grandparents were, the opportunities that we now enjoy. It's quite another to squander those opportunities.

But, ladies and gentlemen, in order to take advantage of where you are, who you are, and what you are capable of becoming, you have to pay the price. Let me tell you of one of the great truths of life that is quite simple to explain. The world is full of people who have the will to succeed. What is required, however, is the will prepare and the will do the hard work which sows the seeds of success.

And that's why, when people come up to me and say, "you're one lucky brother. Good things seem to just fall right into your lap." I tell them that, by the grace of God, I agree with them. But I hasten to add this thought, which has been confirmed over the years time and time again. The harder I work, the luckier I seem to get.

Ladies and gentlemen, you've got to convince yourselves that God has divinely designed and destined you with greatness in mind. You've got to decide, here and now, that you are gifted and that you will not permit yourself or anyone else to view you as otherwise.

Each one of you is gifted. As such, you must be intent on always manifesting your God-given greatness. Alas, ladies and gentlemen, I have good news for you today. The good news that that genius does not have a color. The good news is that excellence and greatness does not have a gender. We all have the capacity to defy the odds, to overcome the obstacles and, through the grace of God, and sweat, tears and dogged determination, pen your own success story.

That's the good news today. That you do not need to be limited in your dreams. In fact, I challenge each of you to remember the words of the president emeritus of this famed institution. It was Dr. Mays who said:

"It must be borne in mind that the tragedy of life does not lie in not reaching your goal. The tragedy lies in having no goal to reach. It is not a calamity to die with dreams unfulfilled, but it is a calamity not to dream. There is no disaster in being unable to capture your ideal, but there is disgrace in having no ideal to capture. It is not a disgrace to reach for the stars, but it is a disgrace to have no stars to reach for. Not failure, but low aim, this is the sin."

So, ladies and gentlemen, dream boldly and dare greatly! Thank you for the opportunity to share with you, and God bless each and every one of you.

A NEW HERO CATEGORY

It is my pleasure to be a part of this splendid assembly and to celebrate the outstanding work of the students here. Congratulations on your accomplishments to date. I join with your teachers, parents, family members and friends in saying— we are very proud of you.

I want to talk with you very briefly about a new category of hero. First, let me tell you about someone who may not be well known to all of you accept for his name.

Henry Kissinger was born in Furth, Germany on this date in 1923. If history had taken a different turn, he would have stayed in Germany and history would have also taken a different turn. But, thanks to the need to flee from Nazi oppression, he and his family came to the United States as refugees, and Henry Kissinger grew up to be one of the most celebrated American Secretaries of State. He made history just by becoming Secretary of State, the first of his faith—and the first U.S. Secretary of State to speak with a German accent. But he also made history by breaking away from precedents, by aware that public opinion was a strong force in the world, and by working about three times as hard as most people.

Did you get that? By working three times as hard as most people.

Well, in a couple of years the man completely in charge of one of America's largest companies, whose major product is an American icon, will be an African American.

His name is Ken Chenault and he will become the chief executive officer of the American Express Company. He is currently the president and chief operating officer, and in the year 2001 he will occupy the top spot. When you hear people say, "don't leave home without it," (referring to American Express), they will also be talking about this African American.
Growing up in Hempstead, New York he played "king of the mountain" and always wanted to be king. In high school he captained the basketball, soccer and track teams in the same year, while also serving as class president.
Like Henry Kissinger, even then, he was working three times as hard as everyone else.

He learned from his father, a dentist, to put his head down, work hard, and to be the best that he could possibly be.

He said that his father impressed upon him to perform at the highest level and to always respect other people. He also told his son that there would always be challenges, obstacles and barriers. However, the one thing you can control is your performance. And that was the one thing that he tried to adhere to throughout his career. And now, by working three times as hard das everyone else, he is about to become the CEO of an important Fortune 500 company, which is one of the largest in the world.

Young people, you need to know that because he worked harder than most other people he was highly qualified for this new assignment. He did not get it because he was an African American, but because he was qualified!

And that is my message to each of you. I want you to pledge to yourselves and your families that you will also work three times as hard as everyone else! If you do, you will be like Ken Chenault—like Franklin Raines, Chairman/CEO of the Fannie Mae Corporation—like Ann Fudge, president of Maxwell House Coffee—like Emma Chappell, the founder and president of Philadelphia's United Bank—like Roy Roberts, head of General Motors North American sales, service and marketing division.

We all know of Magic Johnson, the basketball player. But I wonder if you really know Magic Johnson, the businessman, who is building a high-powered portfolio of business enterprises.

Hear what Magic said of himself in a recent issue of <u>Black Enterprise</u> magazine. He said, "Everyone looks at me and still sees basketball. But I run all of the companies. People who don't know me may not believe that, but if they come in here and want to do some business, they'll find out fast enough."

Young people, that's not being cocky. That's the confidence of someone who has committed himself to paying the dues necessary to be successful. He has worked three times as hard as everyone else.

Scholars and other high-achievers, it is important for you to know that these kinds of achievements are not new. African Americans are just moving to new, higher, and more visible positions of leadership.

Madame C.J. Walker was one of the first highly successful businesspersons when she founded her hair care company. And the list has gone on after her.

In the mid-1970's a man named Clifton Wharton became the first African American to serve as president of a major university when he became president of Michigan State University. Some years later he became the first African American to head a Fortune 500 company when he became CEO of the massive teachers pension fund called TIAA-CREF.

It is important young people, for you to fully embrace the view that you must work three times as hard, even today. You also must have confidence in yourself. You must have the discipline to learn. And you must also have faith in the future. As Jesse Jackson says—"you must always keep hope alive." You see, young people, you need these same qualities in order for you to work three times as hard, and to achieve and have success in your school work, as well as in life itself.

I want to read about the John's and Jane's in this class and this school who will achieve like Ken Chenault, Magic Johnson, Franklin Raines, Ann Fudge and Emma Chappell.

As I close, let me leave you with this thought that I treasure because it came from my father when I was very young. "If you want to get ahead, get something in your head."

Congratulations to each of you. We are proud of you! Remember these words—work three times as hard and you will make it anywhere!

BEGINNING—NOT TERMINATION

Thank you for the very flattering introduction. I am honored to be here and to have the opportunity to speak to this audience and these graduates. I am also humbled because I remember when I was graduating very well. But I do not have the slightest recollection of who the speaker was, or what was said. Since I suspect that you will be like me, that is indeed humbling for me as the speaker.

Sometimes I wonder why we don't call these events "termination exercises" instead of "commencement exercises." After all, this symbolizes the end of your studies here, does it not? You and I both know the answer to that question. After every ending, there is a new beginning, a new start, and a commencement. But tonight is recognition of a change in your lives and recognition of your scholastic success. But somebody once said: "nothing wilts faster than laurels that are rested upon." So the question at commencement is: "What will you do in your 'new beginning' to be successful?" To answer that question you have to answer the fundamental question—what is success? That is what I want to talk about for the next few minutes.

Success is simply finding what is important in life. That differs for each of us. While there are lots of people who are getting a degree like yours, or will have a job like yours, you are the only person alive, who has sole custody of your life. Only you can determine what is important for that life.

I have some suggestions you might want to consider. In this era of rapid change, we need to remember Mahatma Gandhi's statement that "there is more to life than speeding it up." Or as Dr. Martin Luther King, Jr. said, "the real measure of life is its quality, not its quantity." We were all reminded how precious life is with the space shuttle tragedy this spring, and how quickly lives were lost. While we are still committed to the conquest of outer space, it may be that for each of us, the real mission is the conquest of inner space. Inner space is the distance separating what you are from what you can be. Reducing or conquering that inner space may be the central task for a successful life.

According to Sigmund Freud, the central tasks of life were to love, and to work. He was referring to the ability to give and receive affection, and to gain satisfaction from meaningful work. We might add a third task—to learn to learn—so that we can cope with a new and still emerging unknown future. So love, work, and learn may equal success.

On the other hand, success may mean being extraordinary. As Professor Joseph Langlund said: "The significant texture of our lives is made up of a small number of extraordinary responses to a high number of ordinary experiences."

As the baseball season is now underway, let me give you a baseball example. In the major leagues, a .300 hitter makes a lot of money and is extraordinary, while a .250 hitter is not. The difference between a .300 hitter and a .250 hitter is just one more hit out of every 20 times at bat.

I say again, "the significant texture of our lives is made up out of a small number of ordinary experiences." Any faculty member here will tell you there is nothing more embarrassing to a professor than watching a student do something you told him/her was not possible. I truly believe that the inevitable is only that which we don't resist and the unattainable is only that which we fail to attempt. We all have the potential to be extraordinary.

Going back to Freud's definition of success, I believe that to love means more than giving and receiving affection. It also means caring about people. With the completion of the sequencing of the human genome and its thousands of genetic strings, and all our new scientific knowledge, we still recognize that a human being is the most complex thing known in the universe. That is why I believe that a fundamental philosophic or even religious principle can be summed up in two words: people matter!

It is within our relations with one another that each of us must define our success. But caring about people means getting involved. You can't just sit on the sidelines and watch. There is that old saying that 10% of the people make things happen, 40% watch things happen, and the remaining 50% don't even know anything is happening. While the percentages might not be exactly right, the concept is. If you care enough, you will be one of the people who make things happen.

Life is short, when it is all over, you will ask yourself, or maybe your Maker will ask you—"were you successful? Did you make a difference?" How do you measure that? There is an old Irish proverb that says when you came into this world, you were crying and everyone else was smiling and laughing. Live your life in such a way that when you leave this world, you will be smiling and everyone else will be crying.

I like what Ralph Waldo Emerson said: "To laugh often and much, to win the respect of intelligent people and the affection of children; to earn the appreciation of honest critics and endure the betrayal of false friends; to appreciate beauty; to find the best in others; to leave the world a bit better, whether by a healthy child, a garden patch, or a redeemed social condition; to know even one life has breathed easier because you lived—this is to have succeeded."

As you shortly receive your diploma and leave this place, my wish for each of you is that you achieve that kind of success. And that you may be able to love fully, to be involved in your community, to work happily and to continue to learn and grow in the conquest of your inner space.

MAKING A DIFFERENCE IN A CHANGING WORLD

As I return once again to a university campus, I am reminded of the events that I have been a part of during my career in the academic community. There was the "turbulent time," a decade that brought us the Vietnam War, the assassinations of John, and Robert Kennedy, Martin Luther King, Jr, and Malcolm X—and possibly the beginning of the most rapid and unceasing period of change in America.

I would hope that my comments will leave a message for students, as well as business and government leaders, and the faculty who teach these students. Each of these stakeholder groups must shoulder the responsibility of managing change well into the future.

When I was a student and prepared for final exams, I couldn't help wondering what on earth I would do in the coming years. Was I ready for the responsibilities that lie ahead? Would I get a good job? Would I get married? Raise a family?

To the students in this audience: you probably ask yourselves some of the same questions. I know that your careers are just as important to you as mine is to me. I'm here to tell you that <u>your future will exceed your greatest expectations</u> if you put your heart and mind into any job you are given. Use all your talents. You will succeed if you have confidence in your abilities and remember that you were given your own special talents to <u>benefit others as well as yourselves.</u>

I want to share a story about someone who was born on September 12, 1913. Although he died in 1980, Jesse Owens is someone worth remembering. As a student athlete from Ohio State, Jesse Owens represented the United States during the 1936 Olympics. Imagine the discrimination that Jesse faced that year in Berlin. Adolf Hitler had publicly vilified him and the nine other black athletes on the American team. Hitler called them "inferior" but, of course, they were not. That year the United States took 12 first-place-awards, more than all the other 52 nations put together.

Jesse Owens ran on the winning 400-meter relay team and won the running broad jump. He ran the 100-meter dash in a record 10.2 seconds and also set a new record for the 200 meter race. The crowd roared when Jesse Owens crossed the finish line in 20.7 seconds. Millions of people worldwide recognized that he had excelled. Jesse Owens won four gold medals in field and track, and he helped the American team set new world records. His team was the stronger because of its diversity, and because he overcame prejudice and gave his personal best. Jesse Owens and the rest of the American track and field team showed they had what it takes to be "world class."

U.S. companies today are also striving to be world class. Business must overcome many new hurdles. In today's global economy being "world class" is, what it takes to remain competitive and to prosper. That's the only way U.S. business can continue providing good jobs and a high standard of living.

We are all consumers. Because we are, it is easy to understand why people want to get "a lot for the money." We all want the most for our money and, more importantly, we want to provide the best possible lifestyle for our families. We shop for the best value in all our purchases.

Whether we are in business for ourselves, work for someone else, or lead a college, we should never forget that—like us—those that we serve expect the most for their hard-earned dollars. That's what I mean when I say that we must put our hearts into our work.

Each of us must give our best if our organizations are to succeed. If we are not willing to give our best, there is someone else out there who will. If not someone else in your company or organization, then someone elsewhere in the country or the world.

A French author recently gave this analogy: Executives are like joggers because they never stop running.

I can tell you from personal experience that is so true. At each stop in my career, I've given my best, and I've never stopped running. In business or education, the target we call the "best" is constantly moving.

We all want better products and services, and we all must strive to look for better ways to do things, to continually improve and to achieve more than has been achieved in the past. Just like Jesse Owens set those world records.

This century has brought technological change that people could not even imagine when I was an undergraduate student. IBM invented the computer floppy disk in 1970. Today computers allow us to work at amazing speed and exceed what once were our highest expectations. We can use the Internet, or World Wide Web, to share information with people around the world in less time than it took Jesse Owens to run the 100 meter dash.

Here is an example of just how fast the pace of change is in today's society. Research has shown that fast food customers will become restless standing in line at McDonald's for 30 seconds. Just think. That's not much longer than it took Jesse Owens in 1936 to win a gold medal for the 200-meter dash.

Similarly, electricity consumers expect more today than ever before. If a storm knocks down a power line and people lose electricity, they want to quickly find out how soon the power will be restored. Business customers putting in new service or upgrading existing service demand immediate attention.

Detroit Edison, for example, has developed state-of-the-art computer systems to get information from and to there customers more quickly. The systems of that company allow them to provide better quality information and to offer new services to help their customers become more efficient so they can compete more effectively in a global marketplace.

I submit to you, that in order to succeed in an environment of continual change, we all must possess seven qualities. These seven characteristics are at the heart of any successful team.

These same seven qualities also are essential for career success so I want to help you to remember them. Close your eyes for a moment. Picture yourself tasting a shiny red apple that is so good that your mouth waters and you want to eat the fruit to the core. Now picture a FTD delivery truck pulling in front your home and delivering a dozen long-stemmed red roses. I want you to use these mental pictures as a mnemonic device to recall the words CORE and FTD. It will be easy to remember the seven attributes of a successful team if you spell out these two words.

First, the C in core reminds us of our customers (in business or education), and that they have choices as to how to spend their money. How do we show that we care for those that we serve? Do we demonstrate that we are concerned about satisfying all their needs? Do we listen carefully to better understand what they really want?

We all have customers. We all have something to sell. We all sell ourselves. So being customer driven can help you right now. For instance, if you are looking for a job, you must convince recruiters that you have the skills the company needs. How do you do that? By researching companies and finding ones that match your abilities. Talk to people. Learn more about the company that you want to work for so that you can put your focus on how you might help it. Show your initiative. Find new ways to convince managers that you are the best person for the job. After all, in this example, the company is the customer that you want to buy your service.

The letter O in the acronym <u>Core</u> stands for Optimism. No matter how bleak the situation, we must never give up hope.

That message comes out clearly in the book, <u>The Diary of a Young Girl</u>. Anne Frank was a teenager whose family went into hiding in Holland because of the oppression that Jews suffered during Hitler's reign. This teenager's diary had a huge effect on our world. Even today, five decades after her death in a German concentration camp, Anne Frank is remembered for her overwhelming optimism.

A positive outlook can help people change tragedy into triumph. Candy Lichtner founded Mothers Against Drunk Driving in 1980 after her teenage daughter died in a traffic accident involving a drunk driver. Lichtner also, organized Students Against Drunk Driving. These two national organizations have changed the way people think about drinking and driving. They have saved countless lives.

Successful people think in terms of opportunities. They celebrate their successes. They also recognize and reward fellow team members for their contributions.

The letter R in <u>Core</u> reminds us there is no <u>reward</u> without some risks. Successful people take responsible risks. They recognize that certain failures are necessary to learning and growth.

Perhaps no one understood this better than Ronald McNair. A crew member of the ill-fated Challenger, McNair was one of my personal heroes even before he died in 1986. Two years before his fatal flight, he was the second black man in space and as a scientist-astronaut helped launched a communications satellite. Like any champion, McNair knew that "true courage comes in enduring persevering, preparation and believing in oneself."

Perseverance. Preparation. Confidence. Those same qualities can help each of you conquer the unknown.

The letter E in <u>Core</u> reminds us that success comes from being <u>efficient</u>. Successful people value results, not activity for its own sake. They have a never-ending desire to improve. Like Jesse Owens, winners form teams that are fast and efficient.

Now I'd like you to remember your mental picture of those beautiful roses that the FTD florist delivered to your home.

<u>F-T-D</u>. The letter F stands for <u>flexibility</u>. A successful team can quickly change the way it thinks about its environment. It can tolerate ambiguity, team members can navigate and travel multiple paths using a compass if they don't have a map. They'll keep their eyes on their North Star and consider alternate approaches to reach their destination.

The letter T in the acronym reminds us that successful people are <u>team focused</u>. They work together for a common goal. They share information and decision making. They know the business not just their jobs. Members are self-directed; leaders can come from anywhere on the team.

The letter D reminds us that successful teams—like the 1936 American Olympic team—are diverse. Unlike Adolf Hitler who refused to acknowledge Jesse Owens' victory at the Olympics, successful people willingly admit when they are mistaken. The ultimate winners in life <u>admit when they are wrong and they go forward</u>. Successful teams respect the individual. They judge ideas on their own merits. They reward people for performance. Successful people earn trust through integrity. They allow constructive dissent to add value, building on ideas by establishing a healthy dialogue. Successful teams develop people and utilize their own unique talents.

To succeed, companies and organizations today need teamwork like that which was found on the 1936 Olympic team. No matter how well developed our computer systems, we can't continue to succeed unless our employees are willing to put their hearts and minds into each day's work.

After all, to quote John F. Kennedy, "Man is the most extraordinary computer of all."

I would modify President Kennedy's thoughts only slightly to make it clear that U.S. companies today need the brainchild of men, women and minorities. With all of our combined brainpower, I believe American businesses and other organizations will continue to excel just as surely as our country won the race to put a man on the moon.

Affirmative action benefits everyone. Young and old Men and women. All people, without regard to race, color, religion or national origin. We all need each other. The unique talents that people offer us are much more important to us than their differences. We must never limit ourselves, or our society, by excluding anyone. We must cultivate all of our talents.

Who knows who will discover a cure for diseases like cancer and AIDS? Jonas Salk was only an average student in high school who was generally ignored by his classmates, but he went on to discover the polio vaccine.

When the brilliant surgeon Ben Carson was growing up in Detroit, I'm sure that most people never realized that this young black man would grow up to be a talented neurosurgeon at Johns Hopkins University. At one point Ben was doing so poorly in school that his math teacher said she was encouraged when he finally turned in a "D" assignment. When he was 14, Ben fought a friend with a knife and nearly killed him. It was then that he decided to turn his life around.

Ben set out to fulfill his dream of becoming a doctor and saving people. He improved his grades, graduating third in his high school class and receiving scholarships to Yale and the University of Michigan Medical School. By the time he was 33 he was director of pediatric neurosurgery at Johns Hopkins Hospital. In 1987, Dr. Ben Carson did what other surgeons thought was impossible. He separated Siamese twins joined at the head. Patrick and Benjamin Binder wouldn't have had a chance if Ben Carson hadn't pursued his dream to be a doctor.

Much of the strength, the creative genius and the soul of American society comes from its diversity. Our potential is greater than ever. U.S. business will prosper as it recognizes the value of a diverse work force and uses all of its resources. Diversity will help companies keep moving in the right direction as the pace picks up in our increasingly connected multi-cultural world.

In conclusion, I offer some advice to today's students. Recognize the differences between yourselves and others, but never let those differences stop you in your tracks or in your career.

- *Keep going*
- *Keep learning*
- *Keep caring*

Remember the tasty apple, the beautiful flowers and think of the seven qualities in the word CORE and the acronym F.T.D.

- *Don't be afraid to bite deep into the fruit of life*
- *Show your care and concern*
- *Be optimistic*
- *Take responsible risks*
- *Be efficient and keep your eye on results*

And I hope you will still smell the roses no matter how fast you are moving. Join groups that are:

- *Flexible*
- *Team oriented*
- *Supportive of and value diversity*

But most of all, remember the <u>customer</u> deserves nothing less, than your best. And, I am confident that you'll create career opportunities for yourselves that exceed your highest expectations today. Of course, you may not think so at the time because the winners in life—like Jesse Owens—are always looking for ways they can go faster or jump higher. They realize that is what it takes to be world class.

Thank you for your attention and I wish you the very best.

REMEMBRANCES AT GRADUATION

To the graduates, I offer you sincere congratulations on this significant achievement in your respective lives. Commendations are also in order for your families and significant others who have supported you in your educational journey. As I frequently say to students, there are essentially no accomplishments that come our way that are solely the result of your singular efforts. Always acknowledge those who have aided you along the way.

I have delivered scores of commencement addresses during my career in higher education at universities, colleges, high schools, and others. Typically the commencement address is the one thing on the program that does not hold the attention of the graduates. Generally we commencement speakers are urged to "keep the talk less than fifteen minutes."

Because of the significance of this service in your lives, I may take a couple of more minutes to leave thoughts with you that I trust you will take to heart.

Robert F. Kennedy said, "Some people see things as they are, and say why. I dream things that never were and say, why not?" I challenge you to continually reflect on those words of Robert Kennedy as you from this point forward in your lives, because I would assert that you are realizing your dreams, with this activity.

I would also challenge you to assimilate in your thinking these words of the famed Louis Pasteur: "As you go through life, make curiosity your life preserver." Your graduation is a vivid testimony that you have been curious up to this point in time. Keep at it!

In Atlanta, George there is a unique historically black college— Morehouse College. Its most famous president was the renowned Dr. Benjamin E. Mays. He was unquestionably one of the most passionate and inspirational leaders of the 20th century. Listen to these words that he used in the Morehouse Chapel from time to time:

> ➢ *"You are what you aspire to be, and not what you are now; you are what you do with your mind, and you are what you do with your youth."*
> ➢ *Whatever you do, strive to do it so well that no man living and no man dead, and no man yet to be born could do it any better."*
> ➢ *"We make our living by what we get. We make our life by what we give."*
> ➢ *The tragedy of our life is often not in our failure, but rather in our complacency; not in our doing too much, but rather in our doing too little; not in our living above our ability, but rather in our living below our capacities."*

Your graduation today is a clear indication of your potential and your capacity. Let the record show that you will live fully up to all that is expected of you; want what you expect of yourselves.

Reflect, if you will, on the words contained in this bit of prose by Robert J. Hastings. The title is "The Station."

"Tucked away in our subconscious minds is an idyllic vision in which we see ourselves on a long journey that spans an entire continent. We are traveling by train, and from the windows, we drink in the passing scenes of cars on nearby highways, of children waving at crossings, of cattle grazing in distant pastures, of smoke pouring from power plants, of row upon row of cotton and corn and wheat, of flatlands and valleys, of skylines and village halls.

But uppermost in our minds is our final destination—for at a certain hour and on a given day, our train will finally pull into the station with bells ringing, flags waving, and bands playing. And once that day comes, so many wonderful dreams will come true. So restlessly, we pace the aisles and count the miles, peering ahead, waiting, waiting, waiting for the station.
Yes, we say, when we reach the station that will be it! We can do so many things . . . when I win that promotion—when I put the last kid through college—when I can finally buy that Mercedes-Benz—when I can pay off the mortgage—when I can have the nest egg that I need for retirement. That will be it! From that day on, we will all live happily ever after.

Sooner or later, however, we must realize that there is no station in this life, no one earthly place to arrive at once and for all. <u>The journey is the joy</u>! The station is an illusion—it constantly outdistances us. Yesterday is a memory, tomorrow is a dream. Yesterday belongs to history; tomorrow belongs to God. Yesterday is a fading sunset; tomorrow is a faint sunrise. Only today is there light enough to love and live.

So, gently close the door on yesterday and throw the key away. It isn't the burden of today that drive men made, but rather the regret over yesterday, and the fear of tomorrow.

Relish the moment is a good motto; especially when it is coupled with Psalm 118:24—"This is the day which the Lord hath made, we will rejoice and be glad in it."

So stop pacing the aisles and counting the miles. Instead, swim more rivers, climb more mountains, kiss more babies, count more stars. Laugh more and cry less. Go barefoot more often. Eat more ice cream. Ride more merry-go-rounds. Watch more sunsets. <u>Life must be lived as we go along</u>."

Two final items for your tool box of wisdom.

<u>*Real World Advice for Graduates*</u>

- *Ask questions.*
- *Be flexible.*
- *Get organized.*
- *Be a self-starter.*
- *Practice humility.*
- *Learn to be methodical.*
- *Keep your personal work lives separate.*
- *Be reliable.*
- *Keep your work relationships professional.*
- *Don't be a rebel without a cause.*
- *Take care of your health.*
- *Be trustworthy.*

<u>*To Achieve Your Dreams*</u>
<u>*Remember Your ABC's*</u>

- *A-void negative sources, people, places, things, and habits.*
- *B-elieve in yourself.*
- *C-onsider things from every angle.*
- *D-on't give up, and don't give in.*
- *E-njoy life today; yesterday is gone, and tomorrow may never come.*
- *F-amily and Friends are hidden treasures. Seek them and enjoy their riches.*
- *G-ive more than you planned to give.*

- *H-ang on to your dreams.*
- *I-gnore those who try to discourage you.*
- *J-ust do it!*
- *K-eep on trying. No matter how hard it seems, it will get easier.*
- *L-ove yourself first and foremost.*
- *M-ake it happen.*
- *N-ever lie, cheat, or steal. Always strike a fair deal.*
- *O-pen your eyes, and see things as they really are.*
- *P-ractice makes perfect.*
- *Q-uitters never win, and winners never quit.*
- *R-ead, study, and learn about everything important in your life.*
- *S-top procrastinating.*
- *T-ake control of your own destiny.*
- *U-nderstand yourself in order to better understand others.*
- *V-isualize it.*
- *W-ant it more than anything.*
- *X-ccelerate your efforts.*
- *Y-ou are unique of all of God's creations. Nothing can replace you.*
- *Z-ero in on your target and go for it!*

Once again, warm congratulations to each of you. You have (as the Nike commercial says) done it! Don't let this be your last stop on your educational journey. As Rev. Jesse Jackson frequently says—"keep hope alive." Keep dreaming. Keep achieving. Don't let this educational achievement be a final achievement. Treat it as nothing more than a way station on the way to a higher goal.

Thank you for the privilege of sharing these reflections with you.

First graduation ceremony—Bill J. Priest Campus—El Centro College
September 2005

KNOW THE TUNE:

GO FORTH TO SERVE AND CONTRIBUTE

Commencement Address at
Wayne County Community College—Detroit
June 4, 1999

To the trustees, Dr. Curtis Ivery, faculty, parents and friends and graduates of the Class of 1999. It is my pleasure to join the Wayne County Community College family and community on this very important occasion.

Historical Perspective

After World War II, a complex of forces, the pressing needs of those times, and an educational idea whose time had come, gave birth to the community college concept and its realization. It was America's effective response to the urgent demand for more education for more people, more quickly, and less expensively.

In creating the community colleges, America not only solved the higher educational crisis following World War II, but also helped to stimulate greater democratization and popularization of higher education as a whole. In truth, the community college movement had founded a kind of people's college. Probably it was the first real attempt, anywhere in the world, to provide mass higher education.

Wayne County Community College stands as one of those unique creations, and you represent the unique product of this marvelous example of innovation and creativity.

Two Examples of Advice

Permit me to share two conversations with you. The first occurred between my father and me. He was a bricklayer and contractor. When I became of age, and appropriate size, he would give me an opportunity to work for him when he had private jobs. It was hard, hot, dirty work making mortar, carrying bricks and blocks, cleaning up. My father would constantly tell me these things: "I have given you a job that should be held by a family man. Therefore, you must work as hard as the family men here on this job. It cannot appear that I "gave you a job." Always be moving. If there is no work to be done, don't sit down—make some work! When we would be leaving a job going home, he would say this to me—"I want you to engage in this kind of hard work for two reasons: the first is for you to learn how to work and earn money; the second is to cause you to decide that you don't want to spend your life doing this." His final bit of advice, that I still share today, was: "if you want to get ahead, get something in your head."

The second example of advice was a conversation that took place between Harry "Sweets" Edison and Myron H. Wahls some years ago. Harry Edison had performed at the Lionel Hampton Jazz Festival in Idaho, and Myron Wahls had served as a judge for some of the high school music competitions at that festival. Wahls observed to Sweets that many of the young artists had displayed a high degree of enthusiasm for the music. However, they were still struggling with the basic understanding of how the music should be interpreted. They lacked the skill to improvise.

Sweets shared similar observations with Wahls and concluded his observations with these powerful words: "Judge, if you don't know the tune, you can't improvise."

What a powerful truth is contained in those words. If you will really reflect on it, that concept can be applied to everyday life. For if you don't know the tune, you can't create, compose, conceive, invent, envision, devise or produce.

Find Joy in Your Work

I suspect that many of you graduating tonight received similar advice and had very similar motives for coming to college. Like me and many other people in this audience, you came with the goal of a better life, and during your time here you focused on a concrete career: respiratory care or computer information system, for example. Or you lost a job and your next job required more technical training, so on someone's advice you came to college. Or perhaps you had already worked for some years in a position you tired of, found there was no room for advancement or no outlet for your spirit, so you returned to college to follow your heart: to interior design or veterinary technology. Or you finished an A.A. degree with the hope of transfer to a senior institution, and a career in teaching, law, medicine, or basic science.

There are no fraternities or sororities in community colleges, but tonight you must know that you have joined an important fraternity or sorority of sorts. You have joined those very fortunate people of this world who love their work.

Paul Samuelson, the Nobel Prize winning economist, said that if no one paid him to be an economist, he would still study and practice that discipline.

As you go forth, my advice to you is to study something seriously, work at it in that mix of struggle and pleasure that is now very familiar to you, and in the process you become something. In short, you will have "learned the tune, so that you can improvise."

Some of you here tonight, for example, spent 60+ hours studying computer programming and the associated courses necessary to get the degree. But in a short time, if you are not one already, you will be a programmer. You'll share a common bond with other programmers, you'll feel comfortable in their presence, and you'll glory in twisting a term of scorn—"geek"—into a badge of honor. Bill Gates may be at this moment the greatest businessman on the planet. People who know him know that he measures his associates by their ability as programmers. If they program as well as he does, or almost, then he is interested in working with them. Since his days at Lakeside High School in Seattle, Gates has been a geek, and no doubt proud of it.

Like Gates, not only will you enjoy your work, but also your ability to program computers, or design interiors, or treat animals in a veterinary clinic, will make an important statement about whom you are. It will become an expression of our self.

Emerson said, "do your work and I will know you." This most American of notions, the hope of doing meaningful work and joining others who do, is one of the reasons that you are here tonight. To achieve that goal, you have earned certificates, degrees and perfected numerous skills.

So finding yourself with us in this great fraternity, because you wanted to get a good job and enjoy your work connects you to large numbers of college students who give as their reason for attending college "to get a better job," or "to make more money."

In a recent survey of freshmen reported in National Affairs, 76.9% gave the former answer (to get a better job), 74.6% the latter (to make more money). The third most frequently selected answer, however, was to "gain a general education and an appreciation of ideas." The fact that 62% of the student's chose that answer, or other choices like "to become a more cultured person," we have found an education statistic that can still cheer us. Survey after survey reports that despite rising concerns about the vocationalization of higher education, students in college view the ability to find a good job and enjoyable work and the ability to become broadly educated equally important.

The Value of a Broad Education

Now when educators talk about this second advantage of college attendance, they are likely to stress the practical, the pragmatic, because those things are easier to talk about and frankly to sell. Bring us your sons and daughters we say to parents, or come to us young adults (even older adults), and we will teach you to think critically, to learn to learn, to work in groups, to understand people from all cultures, so that you can live and learn together despite your differences, to express yourself forcefully orally and in writing, And all this is true.

What we don't say, because it is a little harder to explain, is that wisdom and the deepest pleasures await those willing to live in the life of the mind. A true general education can only be started in college, but anyone willing to make a habit of study will develop deep knowledge of human nature, tolerance, a sense of humor, a curious mind capable of precise thought, and mature judgment that is perhaps the most distinctive sign of the educated.

I listened recently a group of students from three community colleges in the Dallas area. They talked about their experience studying in learning communities. If educators could have put words in their mouths, they could not have found more effective apologists for this second advantage of education. These students expressed praise bordering on adoration for their instructors who had led them to some of the world's greatest books, films and ideas. One student said: "we never missed class, especially Mondays, because we couldn't wait to find out what the other students and our instructors had to say about the book. I never thought of myself as someone who would read difficult books or have serious ideas or opinions, but I prepare well so I can add my view to those discussions."

Another student offered that she works at the Sheriff's Department, and that the broadening experience she derived from being in learning communities has made her a better worker. She says, I listen closer now because I really want to understand where people are coming from. At work, I deal with people from many different life circumstances and cultures. But when I can't get through to them, I back up and try to explain in a different way. And most of the time I am successful." If you don't know the tune, you can't improvise.

Your general education here at Wayne County Community College is wealth that cannot be taken away. It helps you survive the hard times, and no matter how good our jobs are, sooner or later the time will come when you need to turn things around. Hard times will come into your lives.

When I need to sort things out, I seek the advice and counsel in a good book. I find that this kind of reflective, thoughtful reading, helps me to move through the dark clouds and out on the other side. Louis Pasteur would tell his students, "life always favors the prepared mind, and you must make curiosity your life preserver." A college education helps you to be curious, and it is wealth that cannot be taken from you.

A college education is in addition, the one gift that becomes more valuable when you give it away. So give it away! At El Centro's TRIO awards ceremony a few weeks ago, I heard one of the student speakers eloquently trace her family history to Mexico and to seven generations of relatives who dreamed of a better life through college and university education. She is the first member of her family to achieve that dream. I can trace my family roots back to the days of slavery. Many of them had the dream of education. I was the first in my family of nine brothers and sisters to realize that dream. Most of us here tonight are first generation college students in a country that is still a nation of immigrants. Leo Chavez calls community colleges the Ellis Island of the late twentieth century.

So give this gift to someone else. But don't wait seven generations to do it. As quickly as you can, do for someone else what your parents and friends who celebrate with you here tonight have done for you.

Tonight I wish you good work and a passionate, lifelong desire to pursue your education. Learning is still the most splendid thing this side of the grave.

Congratulations and best wishes as you go forth to serve, to prosper, to contribute, and to give back.

THE FAMILY:

VALUES AND HIGHER EDUCATION

It is always a joy to take part in a college or university commencement. I want to offer my congratulations and best wishes to all of you who are in attendance today, along with my warmest thanks for allowing me to share this special moment with you.

Commencements are events that traditionally have a profound importance for families. Until a few years ago, parents and relatives were usually in the audience—beaming with pride as their sons and daughters stepped forward to receive diplomas that symbolized hard work and often sacrifice on the part of the entire family. That is still true, of course. But nowadays we also—and increasingly—see parents themselves who have returned to college, accepting the cherished sheepskin to the delighted applause of their children.

In either case, commencements bring families together and dramatize their strength, the indispensable support they lend to the diverse efforts of the individuals who are their members. Hence, it seems to me worthwhile to reflect briefly on this occasion on higher education's relationship to the family and its values.

The Endangered Family

Many people have the feeling that today's family is becoming obsolete.

Indeed, there seems to be at least partial evidence to support their view. Census data reflects that one marriage in two now ends in divorce. A growing number of children live with only one parent, and there has been a marked increase in the proportion of people who are choosing not to marry or have no children at all.

Even within what appears to be families, there are undeniable stresses and strains. The two-paycheck household, in which both adults work outside the home, has a better chance of keeping up with living costs, but both parents are left with less time and energy for child-caring and other matters that are important roles in assuring healthy families. Meanwhile, it is rare for more than two generations to live under the same roof, and many social scientists wonder whether young people's lives are not less rich as a result of their lack of sustained contact with grandparents and other elderly relatives.

Then there is the question of personal relations and communications inside the family. It often seems to parents that their offspring challenge their authority and good advice at every turn—almost as a matter of reflex. They worry about what they read that goes on in so many schools and colleges—drug use, drinking, vandalism, and more. From the opposite vantage, their sons and daughters are perplexed, if not infuriated, by their parents' resistance to change. Mom and Dad cannot fathom why Sally has lost interest in her decorating class. As for Sally, she long ago gave up trying to explain to her parents her enthusiasm for computers. Every time she tried to describe what a microchip does, and the workings of the worldwide web, their eyes glazed over as if she were speaking a Martian language.

Our concern for the institution of the family has bred a whole new academic and professional jargon. The old label of "broken home" has been replaced by the more abstract, if less guilt-laden, term of "*single parent domicile.*" *Unfortunately, it is a good deal easier to coin a phrase than to solve the problem.*

Anxiety and Endurance

Even so, we can perhaps be forgiven for wondering whether some of the general anxiety is not just a reflection of our natural human tendency to over-dramatize. Surely, families have always had their conflicts. What we moderns call the "generation gap" used to be considered the normal rebelliousness of youth, in a recurring but hardly earth-shaking confrontation with the entrenched habit of age.

Maybe you remember a popular TV series of some years ago revolving around the weekly catastrophes that befall a supposedly typical American family. Typical? Well, they had financial crises that would have bankrupted many a small nation . . . alcoholism . . . mental breakdowns . . . intrafamily violence . . . shoplifting and various other petty crimes—and that was just during the first half of the TV season! Can you image what their poor neighbors must have been thinking?!

In all candor, I doubt that the American family is in anything like the last stages of disrepair or obsolescence. The most recent of the famous "Middletown" studies which have looked at three generations of family life in Muncie, Indiana, surprised more than a few by documenting a heartening solidarity within the home; increased communication, more religious observance, less hostility, less geographic mobility, and a smaller generation gap.

On the other hand, the family is unlikely to be exempted from the complexity and pace of change that are pervasive in our communities and the society at large. I believe that strong families and family values will endure tomorrow—as they have always endured. But I also believe that the gathering momentum of change will continue to put families to the test.

Values and Higher Education

Education and, most assuredly, higher education, are critically important resources for families seeking to cope with the tests of change.

It is often the case that a certain mistrust exists between families and educational institutions, including colleges and universities. Families are foundations of continuity. Their basic values are steeped in tradition, in conservatism in the best and most literal sense of the word—conserving as preservation and cherishing. In contrast, colleges and universities tend to stand as forces to challenge and change the old with the new—new relationships, new ideas and, not least, new values.

Now, what stance should colleges and universities adopt toward values? There are those who believe that they should rigorously exclude value issues from the curriculum. These people argue that institutions, which bring value questions into their courses of study, are usurping a function that rightly belongs with other institutions—first and foremost, the family—and perhaps even undercutting those values that families have traditionally transmitted and held most dear. In such a view, higher education's examination of values is inappropriate at best, potentially even subversive.

Interestingly enough, there are others who agree that educational institutions should stay clear of value questions, but for an entirely different reason. They believe higher education functions much too effectively in <u>support</u> of existing values, what they derisively call the "status quo" or "the establishment." For these critics, colleges and universities are little short of propaganda agents, indoctrinating students on behalf of the past and giving no place to competing viewpoints or anything else likely to result in change.

I think both positions pretty well miss the mark.
Higher education cannot divorce value questions from its curriculum. Practically speaking, I cannot imagine how it would be possible for colleges and universities to restrict themselves to teaching "facts" without also considering the values by which the facts are weighed and made use of in the real world. Even if it were possible, however, it would be undesirable. While the ultimate human values may well be timeless and universal, the world in which those values operate is a kaleidoscope of change. Whether through the examination of "objective" data or "subjective" values, higher education exists to provide people with the lenses they need to see the world more clearly: not only as it has been and is, also as it will be, should be, and can be yet.

Higher education measures long-held values against the needs of the future, but that hardly makes it subversive. It also serves as humanity's memory bank, a profound force for baptizing men and women into the richness of their culture, but that does not make it a propaganda agent. Higher education walks the middle, and higher, road. Its examination of social and personal values represents a commitment neither to the past nor to some rupture with the past. It represents a commitment to truth—the multiplex truths of experience, reconciled within the unified truth of ideals.

Conclusion

Colleges and universities do not compete with the family or undercut it in transmitting values across generations.

In the long run, the family and the campus play highly complementary and equally crucial parts in that larger, never-ending process that alone justifies and deserves the name of "education." For all of you receiving degrees today, and for all of you who are their friends and families, I affirm that we are united in seeking the same end. Together, we are in pursuit of both a fund of knowledge and a set of values that enable men and women to gaze candidly at the world around them . . . to recognize the things in it that are strong and true . . . and, without rancor or resentment, to set about correcting those which are not.

THE AMERICAN DREAM:

CALLED TO MAKE A DIFFERENCE

Commencement Address Delivered at
LeTourneau University
Longview, Texas
December 15, 2001

By

Dr. Wright L. Lassiter, Jr.
President
El Centro College

*Mr. President, Faculty, Graduates, Parents and Friends of the Graduates—
it is my pleasure to have been invited by Dr. Austin to share this special
event with the LeTourneau University family and community.*

*You should know that my association with LeTourneau did not begin
with my selection as a faculty member for the Dallas Center shortly
after its opening. I first came to know LeTourneau as a child growing
up in Vicksburg, Mississippi, where there was a major LeTourneau plant
there. A number of individuals in my family and neighborhood worked
there, so it was a familiar name. Later I learned of the founding of this
institution by R. G. LeTourneau and his wife. As a result of significant
growth, the name has changed over the years, but it has remained a
school with a unique and special purpose.*

Our current president, Dr. Alvin O. Austin describes LeTourneau as "a Christian university that can make a difference in the world. This is a leadership institution. A place where the cutting edge of technology and Christian faith can merge."

My appearance here represents a continuation of a regular activity in my professional life. As has been true for the more than two decades that I have served as a college president, I look out today and see another "changing of the guard"—the past and the future. You, the graduates, representing the face of the future—individuals in your sunrise, ready to take your place in a world filled with opportunities. Today is a major stepping stone for each of you in what I love to refer to as "The American Dream."

What is the American Dream?

Everyone knows that America is the land of opportunity. Each year, thousands of us, some native born, some arriving from elsewhere in search of a better life, some from families of wealth, many from humble means, embark on an expedition to accomplish something that an institution of higher education will provide. That "something" being a means that will lead to fulfillment and economic security.

While here each of you seeks to further enhance your potential so that you will be able to contribute skills to some enterprise that improves the lives of others. This experience, which has become so common and so emblematic in this country, has its own name—the American Dream.

I must emphasize that no person ever succeeds to achievement of his or her dream solely by your own efforts. Even before the individual is aware of his existence, powerful influences already are helping to shape his/her future. Parents, grandparents, siblings, friends, teachers, colleagues, and mentors prepare the way, be it for good or ill.

But there is one imperative to achieving the "American Dream" by anyone, and that imperative grows stronger and more complex daily. The imperative is education. My parents were firm believers in education. They literally indoctrinated me and my siblings with two themes continually:

- *Education will open not only social and economic doors, but also opportunities to be of service to our fellow man.*
- *"If you want to get ahead—get something in your head."*

Fortunately I took their advice and literally worked my way through a small school in Mississippi, and in later years through major universities. Never dreaming at the starting point that through their advice and example I would rise to become a university business manager, university vice president, and president of three colleges. We who stand at the commencement podium always say to the graduates—you too can go and do likewise.

Education is Endless

It is often said that we are now in an era of lifelong learning that merges work and education. It is acknowledged that in order to make progress one must not only be competent in the basic skills, but you must also know how to think and communicate, adjust to change, and be able to absorb new ideas and transmit them to others. That is a summary of what you have experienced here at LeTourneau. But this is not the destination—it is just a way station.

This is not new. Look around you and you will see many examples of individuals who have succeeded. Their success being the direct result of continuing to learn throughout their careers, so that they could be able to take advantage of opportunities as they opened up.

The Scripture that was read at the beginning of this service is one of my favorite passages. Jabez prayed a four-part prayer that changed his entire life. "Oh that Thou wouldest bless me indeed, and enlarge my territory, and that Thine hand might be with me, and that Thou wouldest bless me indeed."

I would urge the graduates, all of us, to pray that prayer continually. But for you the graduates, please take it to heart. Your being here today represents an example of your territory being enlarged. Jabez wanted more influence. He wanted to make a mark for God. So he prayed, "Lord, take everything that you have given me and multiply it." I say again, "go and do likewise."

Leadership Thoughts

Let me quickly leave you with some thoughts from my life experience that could prove helpful to you as you seek to have "your territory enlarged." In order to be successful and "enlarge your territory," you must develop a style which is best suited to you, and which will produce the desired results for you. Regardless of the type of activity you choose to become involved in, these thoughts can apply to you. As LeTourneau University endeavors to produce leaders in all walks of human activity, these thoughts are couched from a leadership perspective.

- *One of the most difficult lessons for all leaders to learn is to develop your ability to listen and learn.*
- *Leadership is not a popularity contest. Respect is what a true leader strives for.*
- *Always do what you say you are going to do. Never do those things you have promised people you will not do.*
- *Don't be bound by past practices in your field. Never be afraid to try new ideas—to seek new paradigms. So what if you fail, or you are wrong. You learn from mistakes, so try another method. Above all else, don't be discouraged. Never rest on your past performance.*
- *Form a habit of checking on details in whatever you choose to become involved in.*
- *Make a life-long commitment to never leave God out of your endeavors.*

As you choose your respective fields of endeavor, you will find two kinds of people. They are the talkers and the doers. The talkers are always ready to talk about what should be done and, normally, who should do it—except them. Conversely, the doer simply attacks the problem, solves it, then moves on to something else. He or she is always busy. Graduates, which are you going to be?

A Personal Challenge

All of you, in your early years and especially during your years here at LeTourneau, have received as fine a formal education as can be had anywhere. You are well prepared to combine what you have learned here with further "on the job," or self-education, and thus be in a position to take advantage of future opportunities.

You owe it not only to yourselves and your parents and friends who supported you to this point, but also to this great land of opportunity, to reach your potential as an individual and as a citizen. Along that line, remember that as you the live the rest of your life, it is shortsighted to assume that someone else will run for office; that someone else will care for the oppressed; that someone else will minister to the sick, ensure civil rights, enforce the law, preserve culture, transmit value, maintain civilization, and safeguard freedom.

You must never forget that what you do not cherish will not be treasured. What you do not remember will not be retained. What you do not alter will not be changed. What you do not do will not be accomplished. The heroes and heroines of yesterday have all vanished. But while history cites the death of Caesar, the execution of Joan of Arc, and the assassination of Abraham Lincoln, John and Robert Kennedy and Martin Luther King, Jr., it also records the fact that new heroes arise among us.

For your generation, as for mine and for all others, such figures will surely emerge. It may be your privilege or your pain, to be such a person. To become in Shakespeare's phrase: "the observed of all observers." Or it may be your destiny to observe. You should bear in mind, however, that to observe is also to bear witness and too is also an important role.

So I say, get involved, at whatever level. Give something back to this world, to this country, to this state, to this University. They're all worth it.

Finally, I was fortunate in that I found an endeavor that I learned to love early in my professional life. As a result of that I feel as if I've never really had a day that was too hard for me. I've had fun for my entire journey thus far. My hope, and prayer, is that you too will find something to do that you will learn to love, and that you will never have to complain about your chosen field of endeavor.

You see, it is work itself, not the "reward" at the end that makes our lives truly rewarding. As the Romans used to say, "The journey is better than the inn."

Congratulations to each of you. I join all your families and friends in wishing for you the best of everything this wonderful country has to offer. Be a part of the American Dream.

As you move out into society, we are confident that God will bless you, indeed, in your journey.

Education starts—not ends with the diploma!

SEIZING THE MOMENT AND THE MANTLE

A commencement address delivered at

Tarleton State University
Stephenville, Texas
Colleges of Education, Liberal & Fine Arts,
Science and Technology
August 11, 2000

By

Dr. Wright L. Lassiter, Jr.
President
El Centro College
Dallas, Texas

It is a deep honor and privilege to be in your midst on this occasion, one of the most important days of the lives of the graduates and their families.

I applaud this University for its courage, dedication and exciting sense of mission. I congratulate the University for providing a forum where values are symbolized, choices are clarified, priorities sifted, and where, above all, hope for a brighter future is kept.

To the graduates today, you have demonstrated that you have unique abilities in the academic arena, but you must continue to expand the frontiers of your mind. The faculty here have exposed you to their knowledge, experience, and skills with the objective of providing you with the intellectual equipment that leaves you better fortified to meet the responsibilities of your chosen professions; better equipped to more efficiently discharge the duties imposed upon you, and more enlightened as to the important places that you will occupy in your respective communities.

But no matter how well you absorb the learning gleaned from your studies, no matter how determined your resolve to perform in your life work; no matter how successfully you apply the knowledge of your world experience—in the final analysis, the ultimate challenge is not only to make a living, but to make a life. This is the continuing saga of everyone's sojourn.

It is said that if you don't know where you are going, any road will get you there.
To illustrate this point, I share this African parable with you:

Everyone morning in Africa, a gazelle wakes up, it knows it must run faster than the fastest lion or it will be killed. Every morning in Africa, a lion wakes up. It knows it must outrun the slowest gazelle or it will starve to death. It does not matter whether you are a lion or a gazelle. When the sun comes up, you'd better be running!

The pace of change and the dynamics of the global environment that we must function in, underscores the relevance of that African parable.

I recall this incident shared by the late Judge Myron H. Wahls of the Michigan Appellate Court. He and the great jazz trumpeter,

Harry "Sweets" Edison, had just concluded five days at the Lionel Hampton Jazz Festival at the University of Idaho. They had been judges for some of the high school competitions at the Festival. They both observed that the students displayed a high degree of enthusiasm for the music. However, they were still struggling with the basic understanding of how the music should be interpreted. They lacked the skill to improvise.

They both had made the same observation and Edison made this conclusion: "Judge, if you don't know the tune, you can't improvise."

What a powerful statement graduates. What a simple and powerful truth is conveyed in that statement. As I reflect on it, I realize that the concept can be applied to everyday life, and I commend it to you.

For, if you don't know the tune, you can't create, compose, conceive, invent, envision, devise or produce. Throughout your years of studies, here at the University you have been learning the tune. You must now begin to improvise.

The great thing in this world is not so much where we stand, as in what direction we are moving. To live well, you must have a faith fit to live by, a self fit to live with, and a work fit to live for.

Like everybody else, you will make mistakes, but the cause should be want of information and not unsoundness of judgment or lack of devotion to principle.

It is not only aptitude but attitude that will determine your altitude. If you can conceive it and believe it, you can achieve it. And remember that failure is not falling down, but rather failure is not trying to get up!

Now that you have learned the tune, you must also realize that you can control your personal responses to the challenges that life brings you. In the words of one of my favorite sayings, "Winds may come and winds may blow, no one knows how's it going to go, but it's the set of your sail and not the strength of the gale that determines how your boat will go."

The same idea is expressed in another of my favorite sayings: "I may not know what the future holds, but I know who holds the future."

In closing—graduates you do hold the future, so I urge you to reflect on these charges and challenges:

- *Always remain true to yourselves.*
- *The one thing that you cannot avoid getting in life is a reputation—good or bad. Make it a good one.*
- *There has never been a time when our country needs you more than now.*
- *Remember that material things may keep breath in our bodies and give us economic and social security, but only our ideas and vision will keep us truly alive.*
- *Always remember that if the time comes when all of the knowledge of the universe is put on a computer chip the size of a grain of sand, you still get the kind of treatment that you give to others.*
- *Understand that no matter what unexpected thing happens in the future, that it is not what you keep, but what you give that makes you happy.*
- *Always remember that love is the greatest power in the universe. Love is the one thing we know that is present in this life and the next.*

Barbara Bush concluded a speech at Wellesley College with these words that I commend to you:

"At the end of your life, you will never regret not having

passed one more test, not winning one more verdict, or not closing one more deal. You WILL regret time not spent with a husband, a child, a friend, a parent."

You have learned the tune—go forth and improvise! Congratulations and best wishes!

REMEMBRANCES AT THE END

OF THE CENTURY

This induction service represents a special time of celebration for the new inductees, their families and friends, as well as the leaders of Phi Theta Kappa from across this region. With your induction, not only will you the ranks of the leading honor fraternity for two-year colleges, but also you have an excellent opportunity to receive significant scholarship aid when you enroll at senior colleges and universities.

Today is the birthday of Robert F. Kennedy, who was born in 1925 in Brookline, Massachusetts. At the memorial after his tragic murder, his brother, Senator Edward Kennedy recalled that Bobby had said: "Some people see things as they are, and say why. I dream things that never were and say, why not?"

I challenge you to continually reflect on those words of Robert Kennedy as you move from this point forward in your lives. You are also challenged to assimilate in your thinking these words of the famed Louis Pasteur. When he would conclude his lectures to his medical students, he would always cite these challenges: "Young men, there is such a thing called luck. However, luck always favors the prepared mind. Therefore, you should work hard and study. Be reminded also that luck is akin to the wind blowing the shutters on a window ever so slightly, and when the wind stops blowing and the shutters stop shimmering. Ever so briefly, and then the opportunity fades away."

He would also say that "as you go through life, make curiosity your life preserver." Your induction into this honor fraternity is a vivid testimony to affirm that you have been curious up to this point in time. Just keep at it.

Now I want to share some reflections with you from an individual who may only be known by those who have studied African American higher education history. In Atlanta there is a unique historically black college by the name of Morehouse College. Its most famous president was the renowned Dr. Benjamin E. Mays. He was unquestionably one of the most passionate and inspirational leaders of the 20th century.

Dr. Mays devoted his whole being, and totally dedicated his life to shaping the lives of others. He would address the students in the Morehouse College Chapel every Sunday, and also on Wednesday when he was not traveling. Listen to some of his powerful words to his students. "You are what you aspire to be, and not what you are now; you are what you do with your mind, and you are what you do with your youth." As he tried to instill hope in the minds and hearts of his students, these words are applicable to you: "Hope lies in the very nature of man. Although there is a paradox in man's nature, there is a spark of divinity in him that will not leave him alone."

Not only did Dr. Mays challenge his students, he also challenged institutions. I think that this particular challenge is appropriate for today's colleges and universities: "A college must be judged not only by excellent teachers, but by the spirit and philosophy which permeates it from top to bottom."

Hopefully your induction into this honor fraternity will underscore the importance that the colleges and universities that are represented here have placed in those words of Dr. Mays.

This further challenge from Dr. Mays is instructive. "I am disturbed, I am uneasy about man because we have no guarantee that when we a man's mind, we will train his heart; no guarantee that when we increase a man's knowledge, we will increase his goodness. There is no necessary correlation between knowledge and goodness."

Your induction into Phi Theta Kappa is a clear indication of your potential and your capacity. Let the record show that you will live fully up to all that is expected of you, and what you expect of yourself. The future lies before you expectantly. The future waits for your genius, talent, capabilities and potential. Make wise use of the future.

Finally, I personally ascribe to the following three quotations of President Mays:

- *"Whatever you do, strive to do it so well that no man living and no man dead, and no man yet to be born could do it any better."*
- *"We make our living by what we get. We make our life by what we give."*
- *"The tragedy of life is often not in our failure, but rather in our complacency; not in our doing too much, but rather in our doing too little; not in our living above our ability, but rather in our living below our capacities."*

Congratulations and warmest best wishes for the future.

REAL WORLD ADVICE
FOR RECENT GRADUATES

- ➢ *Ask Questions*
- ➢ *Be Flexible*
- ➢ *Get Organized*
- ➢ *Be a Self-Starter*
- ➢ *Practice Humility*
- ➢ *Learn to be Methodical*
- ➢ *Keep and Personal and Work Lives Separate*
- ➢ *Be Reliable*
- ➢ *Keep Your Relationships Professional Always*
- ➢ *Don't Be a Rebel Without a Cause*
- ➢ *Take Care of Your Health*

TO ACHIEVE YOUR DREAMS

REMEMBER YOUR ABCs

- *Avoid negative sources, people, places, things, and habits.*
- *Believe in yourself.*
- *Consider issues from every angle.*
- *Don't give up, and don't give in.*
- *Enjoy life today; yesterday is gone, and tomorrow may never come. But do not dissipate any day on things of no value.*
- *Family and friends are hidden treasures. Always value and love them.*
- *Give more than you planned to give.*
- *Hang on to your dreams.*
- *Ignore those who try to discourage you.*
- *Just do it!*
- *Keep on trying. No matter how hard it seems, it will get easier.*
- *Love yourself first and foremost.*
- *Make it happen!*
- *Never lie, cheat or steal. Always strike a fair deal.*
- *Open your eyes and see things as they really are.*
- *Practice makes perfect.*
- *Quitters never win, and winners never quit.*
- *Read, study, and learn about everything important in your life.*
- *Stop procrastinating!*

- *Take control of your own destiny.*
- *Understand yourself in order to better understand others.*
- *Visualize it always.*
- *Xccelerate your efforts.*
- *You are unique. Nothing can replace you.*
- *Zero in on your target and go for it!*

The University of North Texas
Commencement—1997

THE MORAL DECAY OF AMERICA:

The Place of Education and Humane Values

It is a great pleasure to be here today to take part in this important event in the life of this university and those who will be graduating. It is a particularly personal privilege to strengthen the bonds with my friend and colleague—Chancellor Alfred Hurley.

As the largest comprehensive university in North Texas, the university has developed since it's founding in 1890 into one of this state's, as well as the nations, most dynamic and forward-looking institutions. You have earned a reputation at the regional and national levels in a number of important disciplines and programs.

The presence of this large graduating class testifies to the fact that each of you has taken advantage of an unrivaled number and range of educational opportunities. Now, as you go forth to pursue careers, further education, or some combination of both, I am confident that you will the preparation you have received from the University of North Texas to be an outstanding foundation on which to build.

To everyone involved—students, faculty, staff, parents and friends of the University—I offer my hearty congratulations.

This will be a relatively short talk that focuses first on education and values, and second on certain aspects of the moral decay in the nation.

Education and Values

A university commencement is certainly an occasion intimately bound up with both personal and cultural values. One may ask, what are values, exactly? In the abstract, values are the internal feelings we have about what is good, bad, indifferent. Useful or superfluous, beautiful or unattractive. In general, values are held by individuals, but on the basis of principles common to a group—your family, community, country, culture or civilization. Values are the social codes that regulate our lives.

In colleges and universities, as well as in education generally, values are an issue of virtually constant concern. On the one hand there are those who claim that values are subjective, individual, and irrelevant to the business of conveying factual knowledge. From this vantage point, values have no place in education.

In the first place, to attempt to teach or study them infringes on the rights of those who hold particular sets of values, as well as on the rights of those who reject them. In the second place, subjective values can bias or prejudice the outcome of scholarly inquiry and research, which are supposed to be value-free.

On the other hand, there are those who believe that it is impossible to exclude values from education, and far from being excluded, they should be required. Some representatives of this school of thought even go so far as to claim that higher education should stand or fall according to its capacity for dealing with values. As Charles Muscatine writes in <u>The Future of University Education as an Idea</u>, "Either the university of the future will take hold of the connections between knowledge and human values, or it will sink quietly into the noncommittal mortal stupor of the rest of the knowledge industry." (Muscatine, 1970, p. 18)

These are not new issues. I should like to suggest, however, that they will become far more critical with the advent of democratic society, with its dependence on public higher education for mass audiences.

The Moral Decay of America

With those words of context, I want to talk particularly to the graduating classes, as well as to the larger audience now. No matter how well you have absorbed the learning gleaned from your studies; no matter how determined you have resolved to perform in your life's work; no matter how successfully you apply the knowledge gleaned here to your world experience—in the final analysis, the ultimate challenge for you is not only to make a living, but to make a life. This is the continuing saga of everyone's sojourn.

In preparing this talk I was caused to remember the famed "One O'clock Band" that is part of the heritage of the School of Music here. Music caused me reflect on a conversation that took place between "Sweets" Edison and Myron H. Wahls some years ago. Harry Edison has performed at the Lionel Hampton Jazz Festival in Idaho, and Myron
Wahls had served as a judge for some of the high school competitions at the festival. Wahls observed to "Sweets" that many of the young artists had displayed a high degree of enthusiasm for the music. However, they were still struggling with the basic understanding of how the music should be interpreted. They lacked the skill to improvise.

"Sweets" shared similar observations with Wahls, and concluded his observations with these powerful words—"Judge, if you don't know the tune, you can't improvise."

A powerful truth is contained in those words. If you will reflect on it, that concept can be applied to everyday life. For if you don't know the tune, you can't create, compose, conceive, invent, envision, devise, or produce. Throughout your years of study here at the university, you have been learning the tune. You must now begin to improvise.

The great thing in this world is not so much where we stand, as in what direction we are moving. To live well, you must have a faith fit to live by, a self fit to live for, and work fit to live with. Like everybody else, you will make mistakes, but the cause of the mistakes should be want of information and not unsoundness of judgment, or lack of devotion to principle.

It pains me to reference this, but I must. One cause of failure could be, for instance, substance abuse. Literature proclaims that nearly a fifth of you will become substance abusers. Let me tell you that there is no hope in heroin, no power in a pill, no reason in a reefer, no wisdom in whiskey, no courage in cocaine, and no life in a lottery ticket. Substances referenced will set you on high for a moment, but they will hang you up, take you where you don't want to go, and keep you longer than you want to stay.

During the course of your careers, you will no doubt cross paths with people who will try to get you to compromise your integrity. The one thing that you cannot avoid getting in life is a reputation—good or bad—which shall it be?

In the legal profession, for instance, the canons of ethics both for lawyers and judges make clear that an admonishment can be forthcoming even for the appearance of impropriety in conduct. While this standard, you may believe, is harsh, its objective is to make sure that those who are called upon to pass judgment on others, and to defend those who have been accused of breaking the law, have conducted themselves in a manner that in no way, not even in appearance, calls into question one's integrity.

I urge you to adopt the same standard for yourselves to ensure that in no way your integrity, even in appearance, is compromised. It will require an integrity that is intact, as well as intelligence, to face the challenges of our society and the world.

"If you don't know the tune—you can't improvise"

The challenges of the twenty-first century are burdened with the history of challenges we have experienced in the twentieth century. Wars, world poverty, human oppression, and economic uncertainty have caught us in the parenthesis of time, spending most of it living somewhere between—"Thank you Lord," and "Lord have mercy!"— as we watch the unjust hand of oppression waved like a wand across the face of the earth.

Homicide, fratricide, suicide, apartheid—the words affecting us like the acts of a chemist tossing a tiny pinch of some powerful ingredient into a seething, shaking cauldron where, below the fresh confusion, there is heaving some deep and irrevocable change.

An examination of crime clearly indicates that society fears criminals, but is indifferent about what is done with them. Seeks easy answers to complex problems, and becomes overly dependent upon the criminal justice system, while neglecting auxiliary social and economic support systems.

There is still a grudging effort or interest to focus attention on the circumstances that lead to crime, but I see no real concern developing on the horizon. Instead the cry is for mandatory sentencing, longer sentences, abolishing parole, emphasizing law and order, and capital punishment.

The real American Dream is to live in a society experienced by all of its citizens as equitable, just, and compassionate. But the widening distance between society's "have's" and "have-not's" is a reflection of the gap between our commitments to meeting human needs and our support for specified strategies by which those needs can be met.

"If You Don't Know the Tune, You Can't Improvise"

On the eve of this century, W.E.B. Dubois wrote in his classic work, The Souls of Black Folk, that the problem of the twentieth century was the problem of the color line. His words were prophetic, and he uttered them better than he knew.

No individual, black or white, concerned about justice, liberty and fraternity can stand aloof and remain silent in the face of events we have witnessed in recent years, and in view of the trends that are now emerging in this nation and in this society.

The nation needs a rebirth of morality, for clearly we have managed to become a society morally confused, morally ambivalent, and morally bankrupt. We have no clear and decisive sense of what is fundamentally wrong and what is fundamentally right. The nation's conscience has become muted, or at best, ambivalent.

In short, time has almost run out to make the American idea the American reality. Until America fully comes to grips with its most historic, endemic and pervasive characteristics at home, it will be incapable of coming to grips with the major problems abroad. Racism has been with us through all of recorded history. Today, racism is no longer a problem of civil rights. The issue is now one of social justice.

Social justice has the goal of achieving equity and parity in the access to, and participation in, all of the opportunities that abound in our nation. All of the benefits, all of the rewards, and all of the powers of the total American society.

"If You Don't Know the Tune, You Can't Improvise

I will never give up on the American ideal and the American possibility, and I trust that none of you will as well. This nation stands before the world as perhaps the last expression of the possibility of man devising a social order where justice is not only the supreme rule and law, but also its instrument; where freedom is the dominant creed and order, as well as its principle.

Yours may be the last generation of Americans that has the opportunity to help our nation to fulfill its promise and realize its possibility. Your generation may be the last to be afforded another chance to balance the scales of justice and make them equal. To confront the doors of opportunity and make them open. To seize the chains of bondage and break them free.

This, then, is the time and this is the place for men and women of good will to take a telescopic view of the journey they take, and a microscopic view of themselves. For it is they who demonstrate in their every action and who express in their every utterance, that they are, in the words of Thomas Jefferson, ". . . committed to the proposition that all men are created equal, that they are endowed by their creator with certain inalienable rights, and that among these are life, liberty, and the pursuit of happiness."

If You Don't Know the Tune, You Can't Improvise

Whatever role you play in life, make sure that your support is from the vantage point of knowledge rather than chaos. Make sure that your support is from the point of integrity and not degradation; from selflessness instead of selfishness.

The important thing is that you must play a role, for while not everything that is faced can be changed, nothing can be changed until it is faced. And it is time, then, for discovering instead of dancing. It is time to look for enlightenment instead of entertainment. There is no time for first-class loyalty to second-class ideals.

It is time to remember that you don't use your past to replay your failures. It is time to learn that worry, in most instances, is nothing more than a down payment on trouble that never comes. For yesterday is a canceled check. Tomorrow is a promissory note. Today, however, is ready cash. How are you going to spend that ready cash, members of this graduating class?

Men and women who had lives of struggle and sacrifice gave substance to the proposition that if one is continually surviving the worst that life can bring, one ceases to be controlled by what life can bring.

In closing, I offer these words for contemplation from an unknown author:

And finally, when they tell you that you can't and you won't;
That you're out of the race and you can't keep pace;
That you don't have a chance,
And you'll never advance.

I tell you . . . . .
When they say you don't belong,
That you're always wrong;
You don't know enough and you can't hang tough,
That you just can't take it,
That you will never make it—
Then stand up, lift your head high and tell them
I've trained my mind,
And I got a new twist,
Take everything else,
But you can't touch this.

As you receive your diplomas, remember that you were taught the tune here. Now that you know the tune, the challenge is for you to improvise!

Congratulations and best wishes for success one and all. Keep improvising!

References

1. Charles Muscatine, "The Future of University Education as an Idea" in <u>The Choice Before the Humanities</u>, Arnold S. Nash, editor. (Durham: Regional Education Laboratory for the Carolinas and Virginia) 1970.
2. Ralph Waldo Emerson, "Education," in <u>Early Lectures of Ralph Waldo Emerson</u>, vol. 3 (Cambridge: Harvard University Press) 1872.

WORDS TO THE WISE

Hear this, hear this graduates: Life is long. Did you hear me? Life is long.

People are constantly telling you—and at this particular juncture, more constantly than ever—that life is short. They mean well, but they are actuarially challenged.

Graduates you can expect, on average, to live to 75. Count the years between your age and 75. Multiply those years times 365 and see how many days is the sum.

Now that doesn't many any of those days less precious. Mind you, it is still true that actuarial tables aside, any of us could die tomorrow. It also doesn't mean that certain choices should be taken lightly. But short of decisions that have the potential to create another life (yes, I'm talking about sex), few decisions are irrevocable.

You will make mistakes. Then, if you're like most of us, you will make them again. Welcome to the human race.

Life is a marathon, not a sprint. Even with a college degree, with the pace at which knowledge is growing, chances are excellent that you will return for further schooling later in your life. Whatever career you choose is likely to be your first career, not your last.

Aim high, set your eyes upon the mountaintops—and then watch with bemusement and delight as life takes you over the river and through the woods to a completely different mountain range, whose name you can't begin to pronounce. Forgive me for quoting someone of your parent's generation, but remember the immortal words of John Lennon: "Life is what happens to you while you're busy making other plans."

Expect the unexpected. Savor the mystery. Breathe and take it all in. Life is a journey not a destination.

Have patience with your elders, for whom many of these realities—especially the part about serial careers—have come as a nasty shock. Hopefully, you will be more adaptable and less attached to your life blueprints than they were.

Even as you practice forbearance, go ahead and revel—quietly—in your obvious intellectual, cultural and moral superiority. That's what being young is for, and now it's your turn.

In short, dear graduates: Kick butt, have fun and Godspeed.

DARE TO FOLLOW YOUR DREAMS

An individual approached former Senator Bill Bradley (who is currently seeking the Democratic nomination for President in the 2000 presidential race) and asked if he really liked playing basketball. His response was, "yes, more than anything else I could be doing now."

The man then explained why he asked the question. "Years ago, I once played the trumpet. I played in a little band. We were rather good. We would play on weekends at colleges. In my last year, our little group had an offer to tour and make records. Everyone in the group wanted to, except me."

Bradley asked why he chose not to continue playing with the group. The man replied, "My father thought it wasn't secure enough. I guess I agreed. A musician's life is so transient. You're always on the road. No sureness that you'll get your next job. It just does not fit into a life plan. So, the man, said, I went to law school and I quit playing the trumpet, except for every once in a while. Now I am so busy with other things in life that I don't have time."

Bradley asked—"do you enjoy the law?"

The man replied, "It's okay. But it's nothing like playing the trumpet."

That exchange between Senator Bradley and an unnamed man prompts me to offer these sage bits of advice. <u>Always dare to follow your dreams.</u> You see, how sad it is that the man, and many like him, choose to shortchange themselves by engaging in occupations and activities that may be safe and conventional but do not deliver any satisfaction, fulfillment and joy in living.

Katina Kefalos observes, "The only real failure in life is failing to move in the direction of your dreams." Dr. Benjamin Mays wisely asserted, "To miss your dreams is not failure, having no dreams to reach for, that is the real failure."

Growing up we all have dreams, hopes and aspirations for ourselves. Unfortunately, various social, emotional and practical pressures conspire to create fear, uncertainty and self-doubt. The result: our glorious dreams and hopes for ourselves are forced into the background. I want to share with you five ways to fend off fear, tap into your inner passion and follow your dreams.

- *Let your intuition lead you*
- *Practice the art of creative visualization*
- *Challenge your assumptions*
- *Dare to go where no one else has gone*
- *Tell yourself "I can remake my life"*

Let Your Intuition Lead You

Intuition is a valid source of information. Learn to listen and trust that inner voice when it calls you to act. Explore the possibilities and take appropriate steps. An intuitive step led Suzanne Kind to become a member of the U.S. Olympic cross-country ski team in 1994. "I started training and ski racing when I was 22, almost a decade later than most athletes," she states. Newly married and living in Marquette, Michigan, she began cross-country skiing and racing. At the end of the first season, she placed fourth at one of the national collegiate championships in the women's 10K. Then she began winning every larger competition. The following year Kind felt she was within realistic reach of making the 1994 Olympic team. "But, she states, I questioned the legitimacy of my goals." She thought, "I'm just a ski bum; what's going to come of all of this?"

"Yet all the while, my tuition told me that this was okay, and over time, I began to accept my decision as valid and worthwhile," she says. Kind made the U.S. Olympic team in both 1994 and 1998. "Now I teach, so I've turned my passion into an ongoing pursuit." All because she let her intuition lead her. So can you.

Practice Creative Visualization

This simple but powerful process is described thusly: "In creative visualization you use your imagination to create a clear image of something you wish to manifest. Then you continue to focus on the idea or picture regularly, giving a positive energy until it becomes objective reality . . . In other words, until you actually achieve that you have been visualizing." (Shakti Gawain, author of Creative Visualization).

An individual who knew how to use such visualization was legendary hotelier Conrad Hilton. The Great Depression was exceptionally hard for Hilton. After the economic crash of 1929, people did not travel much and, when they did, they were not staying in the hotels Hilton had acquired during the roaring 1920s. Business at his hotels was so poor that by 1931 his creditors were threatening to foreclose. Hilton was so financially destitute that even his laundry was in hock and he was borrowing money from a bellboy in order to eat. Conrad Hilton came upon a photograph of the Waldorf Astoria Hotel with its six kitchens, 200 cooks, 500 waiters, 2,000 rooms, its private hospital and private railroad siding in the basement. Hilton clipped that photograph out of the magazine and scribbled across it, "The Greatest of Them All."

The year 1931 was "a presumptuous, an outrageous time to dream," Hilton later wrote. Nevertheless, he put the photo of the Waldorf in his wallet, and when he had a desk again, slipped the picture under the glass top. That magazine photo was always in front of him. As he worked his way back up, he slipped the cherished photo under the glass of a new, larger desk. Eighteen years later, in October 1949, Conrad Hilton acquired the Waldorf Astoria Hotel.

The lesson to be learned from Conrad Hilton is: Conceive in order to achieve the life you want. Develop a mental picture of what you hope to accomplish. Have something for your mind to focus on, and it will become a cue for your behavior.

As Rev. Jesse Jackson always states in his speeches—"if you can conceive it; believe it!"

Challenge Your Assumptions

Many of us operate on flawed assumptions. We mistakenly assume that we cannot do more, be more or enjoy more. Challenge your assumptions in order to rise above them. When I was the first African American president of the Student Government Association at my undergraduate institution, I could never believe that one day I would earn a doctoral degree. I could never believe that I would become the first African American to hold a cabinet position in the State of Arkansas. I also could not believe that I would someday be the chancellor a public institution of higher education.

But somewhere along the way, I was caused to believe in me! I challenged those early assumptions! Now, I truly believe that there is nothing that I cannot accomplish!

Dare to Go Where No One Else Has Gone

Be challenged by the impossible. Be the nonconformist in your group. Take a chance. Embrace a risky task. Always be bold enough to try something big. But keep this in mind that you'll have to do it, as I have, bit by bit, one step at a time. But you can do it!
Tell Yourself—"I Can Remake My Life"

You have the power to shape your destiny because destiny is more a matter of choice than of chance. Choose to remake your life if you are feeling unfulfilled or unhappy. Consider the example set by Sheryl Draker. As an attorney in a Dallas law firm, she felt uneasy about leaving work early to see a doctor about a persistent stomach problem. After a medical exam, Draker was alarmed to hear she had a pancreatic tumor. Three days later she arrived at a hospital for surgery only to learn doctors could not find the tumor. "I don't know whether it was a medical error or a miracle, but I took it as a wake-up call," she says. "The message was clear to me that I wasn't living the life I loved."

She quit her job with the corporate law firm and began working as a contract lawyer, similar to being a temporary employee. That allowed her to study for a master's degree in psychology. Today Draker is self-employed as a legal and communications consultant in Austin, Texas.

Typically, she works no more than 80 hours a month, yet earns triple what she did as a lawyer working 60-hour weeks. The extra time allows her to do volunteer work.

Finally, when working to making your dreams come true, always maintain an optimistic attitude. If the going gets a little tough, keep in mind this wisdom from the American philosopher William James: "It is our attitude at the beginning of a difficult undertaking which, more than anything else, will determine its outcome."

Charles Swindol, the famed theologian, author and President of Dallas Baptist Seminary, had this pithy statement as I close—"your attitude determines your altitude."

DARE TO FOLLOW YOUR DREAMS!

NOTHING MUCH HAPPENS WITHOUT A DREAM

When Howard Finney called and invited me to join the faculty, faculty sponsors, and members of Phi Theta Kappa to offer induction remarks, I had two reactions. First, I felt appreciation on being asked to perform a task that I have been favored to engage in before at this college and in my previous presidency at Schenectady County Community College. Second, I saw this an unusual opportunity to support our commitment to student success.

What now should I say to this large and ethnically diverse group of students who have demonstrated a commitment to a higher standard thus far in their college careers? There is so much that I could talk about of a scholarship and intellectual nature that might interest you. For you see, you now represent the elite of this college. You have demonstrated the capacity to achieve at a high level, on a consistent basis, as evidence by your grade point averages.

If I had the time, I could talk about change, and how difficult it is for people to deal with change. After all, we can't depend on those things that we decided on before—the decisions we make today might be wrong for tomorrow. But it is so important that we start thinking about change in a positive way, and not dread change. But that subject would extend me beyond the time allotted.

If I had the time, I could talk about the two-week period when our world changed more rapidly and vastly than at any other time in my memory. I speak of the massive changes in Eastern Europe. But we don't have the needed time for that kind of discourse.

For the intellectual elite, as you are, I could tell you about the importance of ethical behavior. We could talk about the social balance sheet that we must all keep. This social balance sheet is critical because how we do something is as important as what we do. But we don't have the needed time.

If I had the time, we could talk about the critical need for reform in education in America. This is particularly true of public education. I could reel off statistics that would reflect just how much we have retrogressed over the past three decades. I could tell you that if this country doesn't take action now to reform our educational system at all levels—kindergarten to graduate school—our nation may never again be the competitive force that it once was. But we don't have time today.

So what will I talk about? Let me share a thought, which you can view as a transportable tool. You can carry it with you prepare and plan for your futures. That thought is: Nothing Much Happens Without a Dream!

I can recall that when I was in school, those persons who were "dreamers" were written off. It meant that you were not practical. You didn't pay attention and perhaps "were off in another world." But I have learned that this is not quite right. I have learned that it is through dreams that we accomplish things.

The universe of colleges that we enjoy in this country is the result of someone "dreaming." Take this college district, as a classic example. This seven-college district would not exist today, flourishing as a beacon of service, if the founders had not had a dream.

The California Angels baseball team has a remarkable player named Jim Abbott. Abbott had a dream. It takes a special kind of person to make a dream come true against all odds. Jim was born minus a right hand. His parents raised this remarkable man by treating him "remarkably." Abbott says, "I always pictured myself as a baseball pitcher, but I can't remember how many hands I had in my dreams. I just went out and did things." And he certainly has "done things," as the major league level.

Greg Lemond had a dream. He dreamed he could be the first American to win the greatest bicycle race in the world, the grueling 2,000 mile Tour de France. And he did win. But it wasn't that easy. It came about because of an accident. In 1986 he was accidentally shot while hunting. He was near death with 50 shotgun pellets in his body. In that hospital bed, he had another dream. He dreamed that he would live, and that he would race again, and win.

For those who are sports fans, or enthusiasts of human achievement, you will recall that he was successful. His dream came true.

Dreams come true all around us. Lee Iacocca had a dream. Walt Disney had a dream. Stephen Jobs had a dream. I had a dream of one day being a college president. All of the names mentioned realized their dreams.

But for the next minute or so, let's talk about you and your dreams. Today, being inducted into a prestigious honor society, you are living out a part of your dream. But in many ways, it is only the beginning. Now I want you to do something. Take the time, right now. Close your eyes, if you will, and dream a wild, impossible, crazy dream for your future.

Visualize where you want to be, what you want to be doing in five years, ten years, and twenty years. Hold to that single vision, and when you go home, write it down on a piece of paper, and take good care of it. In the months and years to come, especially if you feel you have lost your way, take out the paper and dream all over again. Take the time to do this, and the chances are your dream will be a dream no longer. It will be a reality, and only you—no one else—will have made it so.

In closing, permit me to share one of my favorite pieces of prose with you. The writing is entitled The Station and was written by Robert J. Hastings. Reflect on it as you listen to the words.

THE STATION

Tucked away in our subconscious is an idyllic vision. We see ourselves on a long trip that spans the continent. We are traveling by train. Out the windows we drink in the passing scene of cars on nearby highways, of children waving at a crossing, of cattle grazing on a distant hillside, of smoke pouring from a power plant, of row upon row of corn and wheat, of flatlands and valleys, of mountains and rolling hillsides, of city skylines, and village malls.

But uppermost in our minds is the final destination. On a certain day at a certain hour we will pull into the station. Bands will be playing and flags waving. Once we get there so many wonderful dreams will come true and the pieces of our lives will fit together like a completed jigsaw puzzle. How restlessly we pace the aisles, damning the minutes for loitering—waiting, waiting, waiting for the station.

Sooner or later we must realize there is no station, no one place to arrive at once and for all. The true joy of life is the trip. The station is only a dream. It constantly outdistances us.

Relish the moment is a good motto, especially when coupled with Psalms 118:24: "This is the day which the Lord hath made, we will rejoice and be glad in it." It isn't the burdens of today that drive men mad. It is the regrets over yesterday and the fear of tomorrow. Regret and fear are twin thieves who rob us of today.

Hastings ode concludes with these words: "So stop pacing the aisles and counting the miles, climb more mountains, eat more ice cream, go barefoot more often, swim more rivers, watch more sunsets, laugh more, cry less. Life must be lived as we go along. The STATION will come soon enough.

Congratulations and dream big dreams!

Phi Theta Kappa Honor Society
El Centro College

CAREER GOALS ACHIEVEMENT STRATEGIES:

Write Them, Review Them, Achieve Them

My commendations to the new leadership team of Sigma Tau Chapter of Dave Ralphs, Les Hord and Judy Davis for your efforts in working with your chapter advisors in planning for this induction ceremony.

A special word of praise and congratulations to the new inductees. You have now achieved a major milestone in your educational experiences at El Centro College. As very few things of worth and significance are ever achieved by one's independent efforts, commendations are also in order for the family members of the inductees. Thank you for supporting them as they studied diligently in order to achieve the qualifying grade point average for membership.

For just a few minutes permit me to share with you some thoughts on strategies for achieving your career goals.

The former wide receiver for the Buffalo Bills, who now lives in the Greater Dallas area, James Lofton, was once asked what tricks he used to achieve success. His response was:

"One trick is to work harder than the other guy. The second trick is to always hustle. The third trick is to study and know what you're doing. Fourth, always be prepared. Fifth, and finally, never give up. Those are my tricks."

What Lofton was really saying is that there are no "tricks" for getting ahead. But there are some very basic fundamentals of hard work and planning that can give each of us a competitive edge, if we use them.

One of the most important fundamentals is the importance of setting goals. If I had to crystallize my advice about goals to one short set of three bullet points, I would say:

> ➤ Set very specific goals.
> ➤ Write down those goals.
> ➤ Review them and work hard toward their accomplishment on a daily basis.

Let's spend some brief moments with each of the three points

Set Very Specific Goals

Someone once defined a goal as a "dream with a deadline." Many people have high ambitions and want to achieve success, but they never get around to defining specifically what they want to achieve. It is unclear what specific position they want to attain, or what specific expertise they want to develop that will set them apart from their competition.

A goal gives you something to aim for, and not even the greatest marksmen in the world can demonstrate their shooting skill—until they have a target. A philosopher once said, "No wind is a fair wind if you don't know the port for which you are headed."

So strategy number one is—set a specific goal. Don't be what has been described as a "wandering generality." It's much more effective in life to be a "meaningful specific." It's much more effective in life to be a "meaningful specific," than a "wandering generality."

Write Down Your Goals

The second strategy is to have the courage to write down your goals. Many people are actually afraid to write out their goals, because they are afraid they will fail to reach them. They are fearful that in later years someone else may see those goals and poke fun at them for having such high ambitions.

As Ralph Waldo Emerson said—"what does behind us, and what lies in front of us, pales in significance when compared to what lies within us."

There is a powerful, somewhat mysterious forces generated when you write down your goals and frequently review them. It fixes those goals in your conscious and subconscious mind in such a way that almost everything you do will tend to move you, however slightly, or subtly, toward the actual realization of those goals. Things will begin to fall into places and pieces of the jigsaw puzzle of life will start to fill in the gaps.

Let me illustrate the power of the force that can be released when you write down your goals. A study of Yale University graduates in 1953 found that only 3 percent of them wrote down their goals in life. This included the following:

- Listing their objectives
- Setting a time limit for accomplishing each goal
- Listing the people or organizations who could help them
- Listing the obstacles to be overcome
- Spelling out what is needed to achieve the goals
- Developing a plan of action, and
- Spelling out why they wanted to achieve each goal

The rest of the graduating students didn't bother to write down their goals. Twenty years later, a follow-up study revealed that the 3 percent who had written down their goals were worth more financially than all the other 97 percent combined. Finances aside, the critical point is the importance of articulating goals in writing.

Review and Work Toward Goals Daily

The third strategy is to review and work toward those goals on a daily basis. That enables you to see whether you are on track to achieving them or whether you need to make some adjustments.

It's like the navigator of a great ship setting off on an ocean voyage. The navigator will lay out the track on a large chart, showing all the points along which the ship is to travel. This track will be frequently updated by navigational fixes, showing where the ship actually is in relation to the desired track.

If winds and currents have blown the ship off course, you must steer certain degrees to the right or left in order to get back on course. It's the same in life, where we have to adjust our actions in order to get back on track and realize our goals.

Goals will add focus to your life. They will create activity and generate the kind of excitement you need to realize your full potential. Goals enable you to build a solid foundation under your dreams.

Let me digress from goals to share two other suggestions with this audience. First, always think positively about yourself and your ability. If you don't, no one else will. Even more important, if you do, you will find that in most cases people will take you as you see yourself. If you see yourself as confident and competent, then that's the way most people are going to treat you.

Second, be disciplined, always striving for excellence without any excuses. Set high goals for yourself for everything starts with you.

Finally, set goals for yourself that are higher than those goals anyone else sets for you. You'll never regret it. Remember that in life you must function both as individuals and as members of organizations—as a team member. Dr. Martin Luther King, Jr. recognized the value of teamwork. When accepting the Nobel Peace Prize in 1964 he said: "Every time I take a flight, I am always mindful of the many people who make a successful journey possible—the known pilots and the unknown ground crew."

The Nobel Prize, he said, was being given to one of the pilots, but he was accepting it on behalf of the crew.

Make an early attempt to select a mentor to provide you with guidance. This is a concluding point that I would be remiss if I did not touch on ever so briefly.

In that regard I challenge you to accept a larger share of the responsibility for your lives. There are many things "out there" that could be labeled as obstacles. Never let them slow you down. A mentor can give you guidance on how to overcome and not give in.

There is no royal road to learning, and there is no easy path to success. Here again is how a mentor can assist, if you ask.

Hopefully, if you practice some of these strategies and techniques, you will find that they can assist you.

I close with some words from a YMCA chief executive officer that I like and commend to you:

- "Watch your thoughts; they become words.
- Watch your words; they become actions.
- Watch your actions; they become habits.
- Watch your habits; they become character.
- Watch your character; it becomes your destiny."

Congratulations and best wishes!

ATTITUDE, NOT APTITUDE,

DETERMINES YOUR ALTITUDE

It is my pleasure to congratulate the largest assembly of new inductees into Sigma Tau Chapter of Phi Theta Kappa in the history of El Centro College. To be in a position to induct seventy students into this honor society is simply remarkable. First of all, this is a tribute to your extraordinary academic achievements. Second, it is a tribute to your personal commitment, as well as the support of your families and friends. All of you who are assembled for this program can, justifiably, take great pride in this special activity that we are experiencing and sharing tonight.

My observations are directed toward the inductees primarily, but I believe they will have import for all. Let me begin by sharing a short piece titled "Attitude" by Charles Swindoll as the introduction to my talk. In this piece, Swindoll places a strong challenge before all of us. Hear his thoughts:

"The longer I live, the more I realize the impact of attitude on life. Attitude to me, is more important than facts. It is more important than the past, than education, than money, than circumstances, than failures, than successes, than what other people think or say or do.

Attitude is more important that appearance, giftedness or skill. It will make or break a company, a church, or a home.

The remarkable thing is we have a choice every day regarding the attitude we will embrace for that day. We cannot change our past, we cannot change the fact that people will act in a certain way. We cannot change the inevitable. The only thing we can do is play on the one string we have and that is our attitude.

I am convinced that life is 10 percent what happens to me and 90 percent of how I react to it. And so it is with you. We are in charge of our attitudes."

I really like that piece written by Swindoll. It serves as a major compass point for me and it may serve a similar purpose in your lives also.

Your being here tonight is clear evidence that you have manifested many of the attributes reflected in that bit of prose. Your being here on this occasion proves that you have the aptitude and you have the interest to grow, change, and develop in positive directions. Already you have come a long way. You have worked hard, and you deserve everything you have gained. It was Bruce Barton who said:

"Nothing splendid has ever been achieved by those who dared believe that something inside them was superior to circumstance."

That is what this induction talk is all about. Being superior to circumstance, and it is intended for those who are, and who want to continue being superior.

I am sure that during your lifetimes you have been told that "you will do well, no matter what you decide to do with your life." That is probably true for all of you at some point. But I want to impress upon you aptitude alone is not enough. The defining point is your attitude.

Have you ever been called odd or different? Have you ever been labeled by someone else as strong, weird, or even eccentric? What you may not realize is that you are like the defective oyster. It was the late Sydney

Harris who had some wise counsel regarding the origin of pearls. He writes:

"Everyone knows that the pearl we find in the oyster is actually an ulcer. It is mostly calcium carbonate caused by irritation. Without the irritation, no pearl."

Moving to another point, let me reaffirm that you have already proven yourselves as scholars and leader. But I must challenge you to continue working hard on capitalizing on your aptitude, and you will be amazed at what you can achieve. Think of the power and potential of those in this room tonight. It's clearly <u>attitude, not aptitude that determines altitude</u>.

Probably the most dramatic example in history of what attitude can accomplish occurred in the track record of Abraham Lincoln. Look at his professional episodes in life. He lost his job in 1832. He was defeated for the Legislature, also in 1832. He failed in business in 1833. He was elected to the Legislature in 1834. His sweetheart dies in 1835. He suffered a nervous breakdown in 1836. He was defeated for Speaker of the House in 1838. He was defeated for nomination for Congress in 1843. He was elected to Congress in 1846. He lost his renomination for Congress in 1848. He was rejected for land officer in 1849.

Lincoln was defeated for the nomination for vice-president of the United States in 1856. He was again defeated for the U.S. Senate in 1858. And Abraham Lincoln was elected president of the United States in 1860.

That is a won-loss record of 3 and 12, or only 25 percent. Can you imagine winning just 25 percent of the time? Most experts say people have to feel successful 75 percent of the time to stay motivated. Lincoln is the sterling example of an individual having a healthy attitude to achieve victory. He had to have it! Attitude, not aptitude, determined Lincoln's altitude.

If you need further inspiration, look at what George Barnard Shaw, the great English playwright had to say:

"I am convinced that my life belongs to the whole community and as long as I live, it is my privilege to do for it whatever I can, for the harder I work the more I live. I rejoice in life for its own sake. Life is no brief candle for me. It is a sort of splendid torch which I got hold of for a moment, and I want to make it burn as brightly as possible as it can before turning it over to future generations."

What a terrific attitude! Can you imagine life ever getting dull, or getting boring for a person with an attitude like that? Attitude, not aptitude, determines altitude.

Thomas Edison once said, when asked to explain his genius: "It's 99 percent perspiration, and one percent inspiration" Michelangelo said: "If people knew how hard I worked to get my mastery, it wouldn't seem so wonderful after all."

You can have the loftiest goals; you can have the highest ideals; you can have the noblest dreams; you can have the richest ideas; but remember nothing works unless you do! It is, indeed, attitude not aptitude that determines altitude. The question is—how hard are you willing to work?

Vince Lombardi, the legendary coach of the Green Bay Packers, once gave the following message to his team:

"After the cheers have died and the stadium is empty, after the headlines have been written and after you are back in the quiet of your own room and the Super Bowl ring has been placed on the dresser, and all the pomp and fanfare has faded, the enduring things that are left are: the dedication to doing with our lives the very best we can to make the world a better place in which to live."

If you want the kind of happiness and deep personal satisfaction out of life that circumstances cannot destroy, search until you find what you can do best, what no one could pay you enough money not to do, what you would gladly pay for the privilege of doing—then do it, with all that is within you.

In closing, let me leave you with the secret of life as explained by a certain professor to his students.

Once upon another time, when God was creating mankind in His likeness and image, there was an executive council meeting for all divisions of the enterprise. All the top angels were asked to attend. God wanted their opinion on an extremely grave and pressing matter.

God was considering giving mankind the secret of life. He wanted to know where to hide this precious gift so that it would be very difficult to find, and then only by the most dedicated individuals.

One angel said that it should be sunk in the depths of the sea. Another thought it should be buried in the bowels of the earth. A third felt it should be encased very near the sky, at the pinnacle of the highest mountain, in the most desolate region possible.

But a fourth angel had a different point of view. "No mankind's a tricky breath. Somebody will swim the deepest sea. Somebody will dig down into the bowels of the earth. Somebody will scale the highest mountain. We should place this secret someplace where mankind would never dream of looking—right inside of themselves."

God now reaffirms that this is the choice that he must make, and he nods in agreement, and so it was done.

The point of this concluding story is that you possess this most precious gift right inside of yourself! It is indeed a matter of attitude. And that most precious gift—your attitude—lies right inside of you!

Life is a series of choices. We have the freedom to choose—on a daily basis—between evil and good; between suicide and life; between hate and love; between immediate gratification and long-range goals; and between despair and hope.

You can influence others in their choices. But the number one choice, the choice that determines all other choices is attitude. The choice of attitude is yours. The secret lies within you. How high do you want to soar? It is attitude, not aptitude that determines altitude.

Again—congratulations and best wishes.

ASK, SEEK, KNOCK

How pleased I am to be asked to return to the Lobias Murray Christian Academy for such a special occasion. The Founder/ President, Dr. Lobias Murray, is to be commended for his visionary leadership that has resulted in this being the nineteenth Baccalaureate Service for this pioneering institution.

My remarks to the graduating class will utilize the Scripture passages read by Elder Michael T. Smith as the framework and focus.

I will address the subject of "Ask, Seek, Knock," initially. Then I will lift up two organisms that offer a unique message, and conclude with some pointed remarks regarding the criticality of one's attitude.

Ask, Seek, Knock

Asking is a way of life lived with an open hand. To ask is to depend on someone other than yourself. It is very humbling. Asking indicates the following:

- *I don't know*
- *I failed*
- *I ran out*
- *I can't find it*

- *I'm not sure*
- *I don't understand*
- *I didn't listen*
- *I forgot*
- *I didn't care*
- *I was wrong*
- *I'm not prepared*
- *I need more information*
- *I came up short*

There's an interesting dilemma here for Christians. If Christianity is no more than a system that answers all of life's questions, then to admit any of the above shortcomings is to be something less than a good Christian. But in our own attempts to be good Christians, we undermine our need for God. We want Christianity to work. We want it to exist in a closed system where every question has an answer, every problem has a solution. We want to show the world a neat, clean, open-and-shut case for Christianity. But in the process, we unknowingly shut out God.

Claiming to be wise, we be come fools; we exchange the truth of God for a lie and worship the created things rather than the Creator—who is forever blessed.

That is why Jesus says we should ask. Asking puts back on track with God. It assumes a need relationship with him—a hand-to-mouth spiritual existence. A vulnerable daily experience. In a society that rushes to fill every need, that steals away the soul of a person and offers to sell it back at a price, we need to rekindle what it means to ask God.

As you prepare to leave the safe haven of this Academy and move into that phase of your life where you will no longer have parents to give you daily guidance and support, I trust that you will not fall away from a dependence on God.

What Is Life?

Now I want to shift the focus to the larger question regarding life. John Lennon had this interesting quotation on life. He said that "life is what happens to you while you're busy making other plans."

James Allen in his book, <u>As a Man Thinketh</u> said, "The greatest achievement was at first, and for a time, just a dream. The oak sleeps in the acorn; the bird waits in the egg. Dreams are the seedlings of reality."

The immortal Dr. Martin Luther King, Jr. offered these sage words of advice. "You must use time creatively, in the knowledge that the time is always ripe to do right . . ."

David McNally wrote a book of expressions titled <u>Even Eagles Need a Push</u>! And I want to share a particularly relevant item from his book in an abstract manner.

The eagle gently coaxed her offspring toward the edge of the nest. Her heart quivered with conflicting emotions as she felt their resistance to her persistent nudging. She thought "why does the thrill of soaring have to begin with the fear of falling." This ageless question that other mother eagles had pondered over and over, was still a question unanswered for her.

As in the tradition of her species, her nest was located high on the shelf of a sheer rock face. Below there was nothing but air to support the wings of each of the eagles. She thought, "is it possible that this time it will not work"? Despite her fears, the eagle knew that it was that time again. Her parental mission was all but complete. There just remained one final task—the push out of the nest.

The mother eagle drew courage from an innate wisdom. Until her children discovered their wings, there was no purpose for their lives. Until they learned how to soar, they would fail to understand the privilege that it was to have been born an eagle. The push was the greatest gift she had to offer. It was her supreme act of love. And so one by one she pushed them, and they flew!

And so it is with each of you. You are about to be pushed from the safe and comfortable nest of this Academy. Your wings will flutter in the same manner as the eagle, but like them, you will fly!

Now for a second story. This story features an organism we are all familiar with. A friend told the story about an unusual companion that he had. His companion was the little ANT. He said the ant was his favorite pet. His friends would question him on his choice of a pet. He would offer this response to the questions. "Ant are loyal, and they don't each much. They don't require a lot of care, and they have a great philosophy of life."

Without fail, there would be follow-on questions about this thing called the ant philosophy of life. He would say, "Let me tell you these notable characteristics of the little ant that we humans should embrace." I share them at this service because I want the members of this graduating class to consider embracing them in your lives.

First—<u>ants never give up</u>! They go over, around, or under an obstacle. They never even think about giving up. And if you get in their way you know what will happen to you.

Second—<u>ants carry their own weight</u>! They are never empty-handed. Ants are ready, willing and able to carry their weight in any endeavor.

Third—<u>ants think winter all summer</u>! When it's nice outside, you never see the ants lying around, basking in the sun, 'chilling out.' They don't waste their time in the good weather. When the weather is good they are working and working hard. They know that summer won't last forever, and they know they should be planning for the hard times that will surely come. Even though ants enjoy their summers, they still think winter all summer.

Fourth—<u>ants think summer all winter</u>! Ants know that however difficult winter may be, it will soon end. Winter may be harsh, but it doesn't last that long, and when it's over, it'll be summer. They also reflect on how wise they were to prepare for the winter back in the summer. Ants know that their darkest hour will only last sixty minutes. Ants know that summer follows every winter, and that the hardships of winter will not last forever.

Fifth—<u>ants do all they can before winter comes</u>! This applies particularly to this graduating class. It is important that you adopt and maintain an "all you can philosophy." How much work do the ants do before winter? All they possibly can. How much food do you think ants store up in preparation for winter. You got it—all they possibly can.

So, the philosophy of the ant can be summarized thusly: Never give up; prepare diligently for the future; realize that tough times never last; carry your own weight; and do all that you possibly can. That will make you a better person.

An unknown author penned these words under the subject <u>What Is Life</u>?

What is life?

Life is a gift—accept it.
Life is an adventure—dare it.
Life is a mystery—unfold it.
Life is a game—play it.
Life is a struggle—face it.
Life is beauty—praise it.
Life is a puzzle—solve it.
Life is opportunity—take it.
Life is sorrowful—experience it.
Life is a song—sing it.
Life is a goal—achieve it.
Life is a mission—fulfill it.

The noted philosopher and educator—Krishnamurti—penned these words. "In oneself lies the whole world and if you know how to look and learn, the door is there and the key is in your hand." So my charge to you is to unlock the doors of life and move confidently through.

Attitude is Key

The final and concluding point relates to an imperative if you want to successfully unlock the doors of life and move with confidence through each one.

Dr. Charles Swindoll penned these words in a short piece called "Attitude." Listen to them.

"The longer I live, the more I realize the impact of attitude on life. Attitude to me is more important than facts. It is more important than the past, than education, than money, than circumstances, than failures, than successes, than what other people think, or say, or do.

Attitude is more important than appearance, giftedness or skill. It will make or break a company, church or home. The remarkable thing is we have a choice every day regarding the attitude we will embrace for that day.

We cannot change our past. We cannot change the fact that people will act in a certain way. We cannot change the inevitable. The only thing we can do is play on the one string we have that is our attitude.

I am convinced that life is 10 percent what happens to me and 90 percent of how I react to it. And so it is with you. We are in charge of our attitudes."

I really like that piece. Your having reached the point of graduation is clear evidence that you have manifested many of the attributes reflected in that bit of prose. Each of you has achieved at a certain level here. But I must challenge you to continue working even harder in the future. If you will work hard on capitalizing on your attitude, you will be amazed at what you can achieve. For you see, <u>it is attitude, not aptitude that will determine your altitude</u>.

Abraham Lincoln is perhaps the most dramatic example in history of what attitude can accomplish. Let me recount his professional journey. He lost his job in 1832. He was defeated for the Legislature, also in 1832. He failed in business in 1833. He was elected to the Legislature in 1834. His sweetheart dies in 1835. He suffered a nervous breakdown in 1836. He was defeated for Speaker of the House in 1838. He was defeated for nomination for Congress in 1843. He was elected to Congress in 1846. He lost his renomination in 1848. He was rejected for land officer in 1849. He was defeated for the U.S. Senate in 1854. He was defeated for the nomination as Vice President of the U.S. in 1856. He was again defeated for the Senate in 1858. But in 1860 he was elected President of the United States.

Not a very promising won-lost record. But he is the sterling example of an individual having a healthy attitude to achieve victory. He had to have it! Attitude, not aptitude, determined Lincoln's altitude.

The same is true for each of you. Ask, seek and knock. Remember the lessons of life. Always bring to your conscience the lessons to be learned from the eagle and the ant. If you have the proper attitude, you can truly soar like the eagle. To heights that will surprise you.

May God bless you and congratulations!

THE CALL TO SERVICE

Your participation in this program is a reflection of your "call to service." The entreatment, yea the mandate, to go forth and offer yourselves for the greater good. You are to be applauded for that.

As your graduation speaker, I want to lift up the life experiences of three personalities and relate each of them to your "call to service."

The first is Alfred Nobel, who was born on this day in 1833 in Stockholm, and who went on to make his fortune as an inventor and manufacturer of high explosives and detonators.

When he died, he left his fortune for the establishment of the Nobel Prizes for the advancement of the peaceful arts and sciences, including the art of peace itself.

It is interesting that he is remembered for the prizes and not for the explosives. I would suggest that this proves that last impressions are the most important for they reflect what the world will remember most keenly about you.

What you do from this point forward will have an impact on your "last impressions."

WHAT IS LIFE?

How pleased I am to be a part of the commencement and recognition ceremony for the second year of the L.K. Bedford Foundation's Leadership Academy and the "young ladies in waiting" who will be graduating next year at this time.

Suffice it to say, I am pleased that you have asked El Centro College to be a partner in this endeavor. Together I believe that we are truly "shaping and changing lives."

Today my remarks will focus on this thing called LIFE. I will share quotations and illustrative stories designed to reinforce those things that you have experienced in the Academy and the Gavel Club for the past year.

John Lennon had this interesting quotation on life. He said that "life is what happens to you while you're busy making other plans." The Academy and the Gavel Club have functioned as being elements in "what's happening to you."

What is life? Life is perpetual dreaming. James Allen in As a Man Thinketh said, "The greatest achievement was at first and for a time a dream. The oak sleeps in the acorn; the bird waits in the egg. Dreams are the seedlings of reality." Again, this has been one of the driving forces of this program.

The immortal Dr. Martin Luther King, Jr. offered these sage words of advice that I pass on to you: "You must use time creatively, in the knowledge that the time is always ripe to do right . . ."

David McNally wrote a book of expressions titled <u>Even Eagles Need a Push!</u>, and I want to share a particularly relevant item from his book as the "point to remember especially" from my remarks. This expression captures the true essence of the L.K. Bedford Academy. Hear this story in abstract.

The eagle gently coaxed her offspring toward the edge of the next. Her heart quivered with conflicting emotions as she felt their resistance to her persistent nudging. She thought, <u>why does the thrill of soaring have to begin with the fear of falling</u>? This ageless question that other mother eagles had pondered over and over, was still unanswered for her.

As in the tradition of her species, her nest was located high on the shelf of a sheer rock face. Below there was nothing but air to support the wings of each of the eaglets. She thought, "Is it possible that this time it will not work?" Despite her fears, the eagle knew that it was that time again. Her parental mission was all but complete. There remained one final task—<u>the push</u>.

The eagle drew courage from an innate wisdom. Until her children discovered their wings, there was no purpose for their lives. Until they learned how to soar, they would fail to understand the privilege it was to have been born an eagle. The push was the greatest gift she had to offer. It was her supreme act of love. And so one by one she pushed them, and <u>they flew!</u>

And so it is with each of you. Today you are being pushed from the nest of the L.K. Bedford Academy, just as the mother eagle pushed her eaglets. Your wings will flutter in the same manner as the eagle, but like them, you will FLY!

Now another story featuring an organism other than the human organism. A friend told about an unusual companion that he had. His companion was the little ANT. He said that the ant was his favorite pet. His friends would question him on his choice of a pet. He would offer these answers: "Ants are loyal, and they don't eat much. They don't require a lot of care, and they have a great philosophy of life."

Without fail, there would be follow-on questions about this thing called "the ant philosophy of life." He would say, let me tell you these notable characteristics of the little ant that we humans should embrace. I share them today because I want you young ladies to consider embracing them in your lives.

First—ant's never give up! They go over, around, or under an obstacle. They never even think about giving up. And if you get in their way you know what will happen.

Second—ants carry their own weight! They are never empty-handed. Ants are ready, willing and able to carry their weight in any endeavor.

Third—ants think winter all summer! When it's nice outside, you never see the ants lying around, basking in the sun, 'chilling out.' They don't waste their time in the good weather. When the weather is good they are working and working hard. They know that summer won't last forever, and they know they should be planning for hard times that will surely come. Even though ants enjoy their summers, they still think winter all summer.

Fourth—ants think summer all winter! Ants know that however difficult winter may be, it will soon end. Winter may be harsh, but it doesn't last that long, and when it's over, it'll be summer. They also reflect on how wise they were to prepare for the winter back in the summer. Ants know that their darkest hour will only last sixty minutes. Ants know that summer follows every winter, and that the hardships of winter will not last forever.

Fifth—ants do all they can before winter comes! This applies particularly to you young ladies today. Adopt the "all you can philosophy." How much work do the ants do before winter? All they possibly can. How much food do you think ants store up in preparation for winter? All they possibly can.

The philosophy of the ant can be summarized thusly: Never give up; prepare diligently for the future; realize that tough times never last; carry your own weight; and do all that you possibly can. That will make you a better person.

Finally, I want to share this perspective poem from an unknown author with this assembly today.

WHAT IS LIFE?

What is life?
Life is a gift—accept it.
Life is an adventure—dare it.
Life is a mystery—unfold it.
Life is a game—play it.
Life is a struggle—face it.
Life is beauty—praise it.
Life is a puzzle—solve it.
Life is opportunity—take it.
Life is sorrowful—experience it.
Life is a song—sing it.
Life is a goal—achieve it.
Life is a mission—fulfill it.

This is my charge to each of you beautiful young ladies. In the words of the noted philosopher and educator—Krishnamurti—"in oneself lies the whole world and if you know how to look and learn, the door is there and the key is in your hand."

Unlock the door and move confidently through. God bless each of you.

Commencement Remarks at the 2nd Year Closing Activity—May 2000
Leslie K. Bedford Foundation
Dallas, Texas

Parker College of Chiropractic
Regional Student America Black
Chiropractic Association
Dallas, Texas
February 6, 2010

LET YOUR LIFE SPEAK

Success is achieved through effort, determination and
perseverance

Can you relate to the following truths which Parker Palmer
identifies in his book Let Your Life Speak?

- *We learn by listening with care to our own inner voice.*
- *We learn from our gifts.*
- *We learn from what makes us happy.*
- *We learn from our mistakes.*
- *We learn from our limitations.*
- *We learn from our childhood memories*
- *We learn from hardship and difficulty.*
- *We learn from our excuses.*
- *We learn from our fears.*

Can you relate to this bit of poetry? I read it constantly.

Just for Today

- *Just for today . . . I will choose and display the right attitudes.*
- *Just for today . . . I will determine and act on important priorities.*
- *Just for today . . . I will know and follow healthy guidelines*
- *Just for today . . . I will practice and develop good thinking.*
- *Just for today . . . I will make and keep proper commitments.*
- *Just for today . . . I will earn and properly manage finances.*
- *Just for today . . . I will deepen and live out my faith.*
- *Just for today . . . I will initiate and invest in solid relationships.*
- *Just for today . . . I will plan for and model generosity.*
- *Just for today . . . I will embrace and practice good values.*
- *Just for today . . . I will seek and experience improvements.*
- *Just for today . . . I will act on these decisions and practice these disciplines, and*
- *Then one day . . . I will see the compounding results of a day lived well.*

Today often falls to pieces—so what is the missing piece? Ask yourself this question—how often do you have a great day? Is it the norm or the rare exception for you? How would you rate today? So far today, has it been a great day? Has it been less than wonderful thus far?

Ask this question—how does today impact tomorrow's success? Everyone wants to have a good day, but not many people know what a good day looks like—much less how to create one. And even fewer people understand how the way you live today impacts your tomorrow? Why is that so? The root of the problem is that most people misunderstand success. If we have a faulty view of success, we take a faulty approach to our day. As a result, today falls to pieces.

I want to share with you, at this stage in your professional lives, some common misconceptions concerning success and the responses that often go with them.

We believe success is impossible—so we criticize it. M. Scott Peck opened his best-selling book The Road Less Traveled with the words "Life is difficult." He went on to say, "Most do not fully see this truth that life is difficult. Instead they moan more or less incessantly . . . about the enormity of their problems, their burdens, and their difficulties as if life was generally easy, we sometimes assume anything that's difficult must be impossible.

We believe success is mystical—so we search for it. If success has escaped us, yet we haven't entirely given up on it, then we often see it as a big mystery. We believe that all we need is the magic formula, the silver bullet, or the golden key that will solve all our problems. You can relate to the fact that we have all of these magic diet programs and formulas, books and assorted fads.

The problem is that we want the rewards of success without paying the price. You don't win the Olympic gold medal with a few weeks of intense training. There is no such thing as an overnight opera sensation. Great law firms or design companies don't spring up overnight. No chiropractic practice just magically emerges. There is no magic solution to success.

We believe success comes from luck—so we hope for it. You have heard it said that "He was just in the right place at the right time" to explain away someone else's success. That is a myth just like the idea of the overnight success.

We believe success is productivity—so we work for it. There was this sign posted in a small business window that said—

The 57 Rules of Success. #1 Deliver the good. #2—The other 56 don't matter. There is something to be said for working hard and producing results that feel very rewarding. But seeing hard work as success is one-dimensional.

We believe success comes from an opportunity—so we wait for it. Many of the people who work very hard yet don't seem to get anywhere believe that the only thing they need is a break. Their motto begins with the words "if only."

The truth is that people who do nothing more than wait for an opportunity won't be ready to capitalize on one if it does appear. Basketball legend John Wooden said: "When opportunity comes, it's too late to prepare." An opportunity may help you, but it won't guarantee your success.

We believe success comes from leverage—so we power up for it. Some people associate success with power. The industrialist Andrew Carnegie once asserted: "Success is the power with which to acquire whatever one demands of life without violating the rights of others." Many people take their view of success and power one step further, assuming that successful people have taken advantage of others to get where they are. So to get what they want, they look for an angle to exploit or for leverage over someone else. You cannot force your way to success.

We believe success comes from connections—so we network for it. There are people who believe that if they just had the connections they would have it made. That is faulty thinking.

We believe success comes from recognition—so we strive for it. In your profession, is there a sure sign that you've made it? Listen to this story. France is a nation of food lovers where chefs receive the highest honors. One of the highest marks of recognition is a three star rating for his restaurant from the Michelin guide. There are only twenty-five such restaurants in all of France. One of them is an establishment in the Burgundy region owned by Bernard Loiseau called the Cote' d'Or.

For decades the chef was said to have been so obsessed with creating the perfect restaurant and receiving the highest award by Michelin. He worked harder and harder and in 1981 received the two-star rating award. He perfected each dish on his menu. He improved the service of the restaurant. He went $5 million in debt to improve and expand his facility. Finally in 1991, he received his third star. He had accomplished what only a handful of others could.

He once said, "we are selling dreams. We are merchants of happiness." But the recognition he received did not keep him happy. In the spring of 2003, after the lunch service, he committed suicide by shooting himself. He didn't warn anyone, nor did he leave a note. Some say he was disconsolate because his rating in another restaurant guide had fallen from nineteen to seventeen (out of twenty). Others described him as a manic depressive. No one will ever know why he killed himself, but we can be sure that the great recognition he had received in his profession wasn't enough for him.

We believe success is an event—so we schedule it. Real, sustainable change and growth in life, and your profession doesn't happen in a moment. It's a process.

As I said at the beginning of this talk—today matters. Many people miss that point—you ask me, what do you mean by that? That is true for these reasons:

- *We over exaggerate yesterday. It may sound trite, but today is the only time you have. It's too late for yesterday. And you can't depend on tomorrow. That's why today matters.*
- *We overestimate tomorrow.*
- *We underestimate today.*

Make the Decision One . . .
Then Manage it Daily

You will learn that there are only a handful of important decisions people need to make in their entire lifetimes. Does that surprise you? Most people complicate life and get bogged down in decision making. Successful people make right decisions early and manage those decisions daily. The earlier you make those right decisions and the longer you manage them, the more successful you can become. The people who neglect to make those decisions and to manage them well often look back on their lives with pain and regret—no matter how much talent they possessed or how many opportunities they once had.

Regret in the End

A classic example of such a person was Oscar Wilde. A poet, playwright, novelist, and critic. Wilde was a man of unlimited potential. Born in 1854, he won scholarships and was educated in Britain's best schools. He excelled in Greek, winning the Gold Medal at Trinity College for his studies. He was awarded the Newdigate Prize and was honored as "First in Greats" at Oxford. His plays were popular, earned him lots of money, and he was the toast of London. His talent seemed limitless.

Yet at the end of his life, he was broken and miserable. His wanton life landed him in prison. From jail he wrote a perspective on his life. In it, he said these words.

"I must say to myself that I ruined myself, and that nobody great or small can be ruined except by his own hand. I am quite ready to say so. I am trying to say so, though they may not think it at the present moment. This pitiless indictment I bring without pity against myself. Terrible as was what the world did to me, what I did to myself was far more terrible still.

I was a man who stood in symbolic relations to the art and culture of my age. I had realized this for myself at the very dawn of my manhood, and had forced my age to realize it afterwards. Few men hold such a position in their own lifetime, and have it so acknowledged. It is usually discerned, if discerned at all, by the historian or the critic, long after both the man and his age have passed away. With me it was different. I felt it myself, and made others feel it. Byron was a symbolic figure, but his relations were to the passion of his age and its weariness of passion. Mine were to something more noble, more permanent, of more vital issue, of larger scope.

The gods had given me almost everything. But I let myself be lured into long spells of senseless and sensual ease. I amused myself with being a dandy, a man of fashion. I surrounded myself with the smaller natures and the meaner minds. I became the spendthrift of my own genius, and to waste an eternal youth gave me a curious joy. Tired of being on the heights, I deliberately went to the depths in search for new sensation. What the paradox was to me in the sphere of thought, perversity became to me in the sphere of passion. Desire, at the end, was a malady, or madness, or both. I grew careless of the lives of others. I took pleasure where it pleased me, and passed on. I forgot that every little action of the common day makes or unmakes character, and that therefore what one has done in the secret chamber one has some day to cry aloud on the housetop. I ceased to be lord over myself. I allowed pleasure to dominate me. I ended in horrible disgrace."

By the time Wilde saw where his inattention to the day was going to land him, it was too late. He lost his family, his fortune, his self-respect, and even his will to live. He died bankrupt and broken at age forty-six.

Concluding Thoughts

I believe that everyone has the power to impact the outcome of his life. The way to do it is to focus on today. Benjamin Franklin rightly observed, "One today is worth two tomorrows; what I am to be, I am now becoming." You can make a good day. In fact, you can make it a masterpiece

Today is the only time we have within our grasp, yet many people let it slip through their fingers. They recognize neither today's value nor its potential.

Dale Witherington wrote a poem he called "The Lifebuilder's Creed. In part this is what it says:

"Today is the most important day of my life.
Yesterday with its successes and victories, struggles and failures is gone forever.
The past is past. Done. Finished.
I cannot relive it. I cannot go back and change it.
But I will learn from it and improve my Today.

Today. This moment. NOW.
It is God's gift to me and it is all that I have.

Tomorrow with all its joys and sorrows, triumphs and troubles isn't here yet.
Indeed, tomorrow may never come.
Therefore, I will not worry about tomorrow.

Today is what God has entrusted to me.
It is all that I have. I will do my best in it.
I will demonstrate the best in me in it—
My character, giftedness, and abilities—
To my family and friends, clients and associates.
I will identify those things that are most important to do Today,
And those things I will do until they are done.
And when this day is done
I will look back with satisfaction at that which I accomplished.

Then, and only then, will I plan my tomorrow,
Looking to improve upon Today, with God's help.
Then I shall go to sleep in peace—content."

Closing Thoughts—Continued

If we want to do something with our lives, then we must focus on today. That's where tomorrow's success lies. But, you ask, how do you make today a great day instead of one that falls to pieces? The secret of your success is determined by your daily agenda.

When I refer to daily agenda, I don't mean your to-do list. Nor am I asking you to adopt a particular kind of calendar or computer program to manage your time.

Successful people make right decisions early and manage those decisions daily. The earlier you make those right decisions and the longer you manage them, the more successful you can become. The people who neglect to make those decisions and to manage them well often look back on their lives with pain and regret—no matter how much talent they possessed or how many opportunities they once had.

Food for Thought

Let me conclude with the sharing of one of my weekly commentaries to my staff in the Dallas County Community College District. The words in this writing are instructive.

I am your constant companion.
I am your greatest asset or heaviest burden.
I will push up to success or down to disappointment.
I am at your command.
Half the things you do might just as well be turned over to me,
for I can do them quickly, correctly, and profitably.

I am easily managed; just be firm with me.
Those who are great, I have made great.
Those who are failures, I have made them failures.
I am not a machine, though I work with the precision of a
machine and the intelligence of a person.
You can run me for profit, or you can run me for ruin.
Show me how you want it done. Educate me. Train me.
Lead me. Reward me.
And I will then—do it automatically.
I am your servant.
Who am I?
I am a habit.

All great leaders share a common belief, which they practice and also pass on to others. If you make good habits, good habits will make you. This wisdom has been around since ancient times. In fact, it was Aristotle who said, "Excellence is not an act—it's a habit."

Here's the point. Habits, be they good or bad, are difficult to break. Therefore, the challenge for all persons in an organization is to determine the good habits that will be the drivers for success. Once the desired habits are identified, good training and continual reinforcement are critical in making them part of who you are. This is food for thought and for you in this Parker College program, it starts with how you address TODAY.

I have enjoyed being with you and I trust that this will be a profitable weekend for you at Parker College.

Dr. Wright L. Lassiter, Jr., Trustee
Parker College of Chiropractic
Chancellor—Dallas County Community College District

A COLLECTION OF EXPRESSSIONS

One of my habits is to collect expressions from others that connect with me. For this week's commentary I am sharing some from recent collections.

"The greatest pleasure in life is doing what people say can't be done." (Northern Trust Banking advertisement)

"Daring ideas are like chessmen moved forward; they may be beaten, but they may start a winning game." (Goethe)

"I tell them that if you stay committed, your dreams can come true. I'm living proof of it. I left home at 17 and had nothing but rejections for 25 years. I wrote more than 20 screenplays, but I never gave up." (Michael Blake, author of Dances with Wolves)

"Chuck Yeager, on his first flight as a passenger, threw up all over the back seat. He vowed never to get back up again—yet later became the first man to break the sound barrier." (Think and Grow Rich Newsletter)

"You are in charge of your own attitude—whatever others do or circumstances you face. The only person you can control is yourself. Worry more about your attitude than your aptitude or lineage." (Marian Wright Edleman in The Measure of Our Success)

"Luck? I don't know anything about luck. I've never banked on it, and I'm afraid of people who do. Luck to me is something else: hard work—and realizing what is opportunity and what isn't." (Lucille Ball)

"Try not to become a success, but rather try to become a man of value." (Albert Einstein)

"The most exhausting thing in life, I have discovered, is insincerity." (Anne Morrow Lindbergh)

"You may have to fight a battle more than once to win it." (Margaret Thatcher)

"Persistence is what makes the impossible, possible, the possible likely, and he likely definite." (Robert Half)

"Trust your instincts. Your mistakes might as well as your own instead of someone else's." (Billy Winder)

"Whatever your life's work is, do it well. A man should do his job so well that the living, the dead, and the unborn could do it no better." (Martin Luther King, Jr.)

"Bravery is the capacity to perform properly even when scared half to death." (General Omar Bradley)

"What we call evil is simply ignorance bumping is head in the dark." (Henry Ford)

"Courage is not limited to the battlefield or the Indianapolis 500 or bravely catching a thief in your house. The real tests of courage are much quieter. They are the inner tests, like remaining faithful when nobody's looking, like enduring pain when the room is empty, like standing alone when you're misunderstood." (Charles Swindoll)

"It takes a lot of things to prove you are smart, but only one thing to prove you are ignorant." (Don Herold, humorist)

Many may have heard the expression, "try it, you may like it." Why not practice keeping your own list of favorite expressions and sayings.

SEIZING THE MOMENT AND THE MANTLE:

A REPRISE IN 2011

President Mancini, members of the Board of Trustees, distinguished members of the faculty, administration, staff, guests and friends, and most important—the members of the graduating class, it is an honor to have the privilege of addressing you.

It would be difficult for me to accurately count the number of times that I have either delivered a commencement address, or heard one delivered. I believe that it would approach one hundred. On such occasions as this, there are certain things that must be said. We know that because there are certain things that you will typically hear. It has been asserted that your degree is invalid, and your tuition is refundable, unless the address includes each of the following:

> ➤ Graduation is not an end, but a beginning.
> ➤ Seize the day.
> ➤ As I look upon a sea of shining, smiling faces, I am filled with hope.
> ➤ You are the leaders of the future.
> ➤ Your generation faces unique challenges, and finally
> ➤ The future belongs to you.

Congratulations! You have just heard a legally sufficient commencement address. The diplomas that you are soon to receive have been activated. However, I have been allotted about seventeen minutes remaining for this address, and I want to fully discharge my task.

I applaud this university for its courage, dedication and exciting sense of mission. I further congratulate the University for providing a forum where values are symbolized, choices are clarified, and priorities sifted and, where above all, hope for a brighter future is kept.

To the graduating class, you have demonstrated that you have unique abilities, and you have worked hard to expand the frontiers of your mind. That task must not stop with your experience here. The faculty here has exposed you to their knowledge, experience, and skills with the objective of providing you with the intellectual equipment that enables you to be fortified to meet the responsibilities of your chosen profession.

However, no matter how well you absorbed the learning gleaned from your studies, no matter how determined your resolve to perform in your life's work, no matter how successfully you apply the knowledge acquired, in the final analysis, the ultimate challenge is not only to make a living, but to make a life. This is the continuing saga of everyone's sojourn.

It has been my experience that graduates rarely remember the commencement speaker or what his or her topic was. My personal experience with this activity confirms that stories do register and remain with those who graduate. Therefore, I will share a few stories to encourage and empower you as you go forth.

It is said that if you don't know where you are going, any road will get you there. To illustrate this point in my first story, I share this African parable with you.

Every morning in Africa, a gazelle wakes up; it knows it must run faster than the fastest lion or it will be killed. Every morning in Africa, a lion wakes up. It knows it must outrun the slowest gazelle or it will not have a meal for that day. The moral of the story is, it does not matter whether you are a lion or a gazelle, when the sun comes up, you'd better be running. Story #1.

I recall this incident shared by the late Judge Myron H. Wahls of the Michigan Appellate Court. He and the great jazz trumpeter, Harry "Sweets" Edison, had just concluded five days at the Lionel Hampton Jazz Festival at the University of Idaho. They had been judges for some of the high school competition. They both observed that the students displayed a high degree of enthusiasm for the music. However, they were still struggling with the basic understanding of how the music should be interpreted. They lacked the skill to improvise.

They both had made the same observation and Edison made this statement: "Judge, if you don't know the tune, you can't improvise."

What a powerful statement to this graduating class. For if you don't know the tune, you cannot create, compose, conceive, invent, envision, devise, or produce. Throughout your time at Parker University you have been learning the tools of the healing arts. You must now begin to improvise in a variety of new settings that you will face and encounter.

Now that you have learned the tune, you must all realize that you can control your personal responses to the challenges that life brings you. The words from one of my favorite sayings are offered as a motivating point for you: "Winds may come and winds may blow, no one knows how it's going to go, but it's the set of your sail, and not the strength of the gale that determines how your boat will go." Story #2.

Once upon a time, in the dark of night, a child looked up at a star and reached for it. Then the child began to weep. The star asked, "Why are you weeping?" The child said, "Because I want to touch you, but you are too far away." The star answered, "Child, just by reaching as high as you have, you have become a star yourself."

Today, this sanctuary is full of stars. Graduates, your diploma will make you a star. Be proud to be a star. But don't be proud for too long. For this day will end soon. Tomorrow, you will wake up to the world away from this university. And the world won't be calling you stars any more.

In fact, the world won't be calling you anything. Instead, it will be asking. It will be asking for the same thing that the world always asks for. It will be asking for more. That is what being a star is all about. To be a star is to be asked for more.

The legendary baseball player for the Pittsburgh Pirates, Ralph Kiner, was a star. He hit enough home runs in his career to be named to baseball's Hall of Fame. But, on the day Ralph hit his final home run; he made three errors and cost his team the game.

As he left the field at the end of that game, the fans booed him. When Ralph approached the dugout, he turned to a teammate and said, "Boy, do they have a short memory!"

The world is like those baseball fans—it has a short memory. The world never stops asking for more. It will never stop asking for more from you. But that's all right. You have been well prepared at Parker University to follow the example of the supreme leader, and be prepared to give more. Story #3.

Now I want you to hear the story about Kyle and another young man that he met at a pivotal time in his life. This is the story of Kyle's new-found friend.

One day, when I was a freshman in high school, I saw a kid from my class who was walking home from school. His name was Kyle. It looked like he was carrying all of his books. I thought to myself, "Why would anyone bring home all his books on a Friday? He must really be a nerd."

I had quite a weekend planned with parties and a football game with my friends on Saturday. So I shrugged my shoulders and went on. As I was walking, I saw a bunch of kids running toward him. They ran at him, knocking all his books out of his arms, and tripping him so that he landed in the dirt.

His glasses went flying, and I saw them land in the grass about ten feet from him. He looked up and I saw this terrible sadness in his eyes. My heart went out to him. So I jogged over to him, and as he crawled around looking for his glasses, I saw a tear in his eye. As I handed him his glasses, I said, "Those guys are jerks. They really should get a life." He looked at me and said, "Hey, thanks."

There was a big smile on his face. It was one of those smiles that showed real gratitude. I helped him pick up his books, and asked him where he lived. As it turned out, he lived near me, so I asked him why I had never seen him before.

He said that he had gone to a private school before. As a result, I would have not hung out with a private school before. We talked all the way home, and I carried some of his books. He turned out to be a pretty cool kid. I asked him if he wanted to play a little football with my friends. He said yes. We hung out all weekend and the more I got to know Kyle, the more I liked him, and my friends thought the same of him.

Monday morning came, and there was Kyle with the huge stack of books again. I stopped him and said, "Boy, you are going to really build some serious muscles with this pile of books every day!" He just laughed and handed me half the books.

Over the next four years, Kyle and I became best friends. When we were seniors, we began to think about college. Kyle decided on Georgetown, and I was going to Duke. I knew that we would always be friends, that the miles would never be a problem. He was going to be a doctor, and I was going for business on a football scholarship.

Kyle was valedictorian of our class. I teased him all the time about being a nerd. He had to prepare a speech for graduation, I was glad it wasn't me have to get up there and speak.

Graduation day came and I saw Kyle. He looked great. He was one of those guys that really found himself during high school. He filled out and actually looked good in glasses. He had more dates than I had and all the girls loved him. Boy, sometimes I was jealous. Today on graduation day was one of those times.

I could see that he was nervous about his speech. So I smacked him on the back and said, "Hey, big guy, you'll be great!" He looked at me with one of those really grateful looks and smiled. "Thanks," he said.

As he started his speech, he cleared his throat, and began. "Graduation is a time to thank those who helped you make it through four years. Your parents, teaches, siblings, maybe a coach; but mostly your friends. I am here to tell all of you that being a friend to someone is the best gift you could give them. I am going to tell you a story."

I just looked at my friend with disbelief as he told the story of the first day we met. He had planned to kill himself over the weekend. He talked of how he had cleaned out his locker so his mother wouldn't have to do it later, and he was carrying all of his stuff home.

He looked hard at me and gave me a little smile. "Thankfully, I was saved. My friend saved me from doing the unspeakable." I heard a gasp go through the crowd as this handsome, popular boy told us all about his weakest moment. I saw his parents looking at me and smiling that same grateful smile.

Not until that moment did I realize the depth of what he and I had experienced. The message in the Kyle story, and for each of you, is that you should never underestimate the power of your actions. With one small gesture, as a doctor, you can change a person's life. For better or worse. The Creator put us all in each other's lives to impact one another. Frederick Douglas said, "It's easier to build strong children than to repair broken men."

Now for the final story, and I will take my seat. The story is about an old man who lived in a small village. He was the poorest man in the village, but he owned the most beautiful white stallion. And the king had offered him a small fortune for it.

After a terribly harsh winter, during which the old man and his family nearly starved, the townspeople came to visit him: "Old man, you can hardly afford to feed your family. Sell the stallion," they said. "You will be rich, if you do not, you are a fool." 'It's too early to tell,' replied the old man.

A few months later, the old man woke up to find that the while stallion had run away. Once again, the townspeople came, and they said to the old man, "See if you had sold the king your horse, you would be rich. Now you have nothing! You are a fool!" "It's too early to tell," replied the old man again.

Two weeks later, the white stallion came back, and along with it came three other white stallions.

"Old man," the townspeople said, "We are the fools! Now you can sell the stallion to the king and you will still have three stallions left. You are smart." "It's too early to tell," said the old man again.

The following week, the old man's only son was breaking in one of the white stallions and was thrown, crushing both his legs. To be expected, the townspeople came to visit the old man, "Old man, if you had just told the stallion to the king, you'd be rich, and your son would not be crippled. You are a fool!"

The next month, war broke out with the neighboring village. All of the young men in the village were sent into battle. All were killed.

The townspeople came and they cried to the old man: "We have lost our sons. You are the only one who has not. If you had sold your stallion to the king, your son, like ours, would be dead. You are so smart!"

The essence of that story is that the old man was smart. He was smart because he knew that life is a journey. He did not know where that journey was leading him. He only knew that if he listened to his heart—his own inner voice, and not the voices of others who may call him a fool—he would be making the right decisions for his journey.

You are also on a journey graduates. Today, you don't know where it is taking you. Yu have already made many important decisions, and there are many more that lie in front of you. Practice listening to your inner voice.

Concluding Words

I hope that my stories will be helpful and insightful. This graduation ceremony and the diploma that you will receive tells the world that you are ready to move forward to the next step in your lives. You have passed through an important part of the learning process. If it has been completely successful, the main thing it has taught you is how much more there is to learn.

As I close, keep this final thought in your consciousness as you continue to dare to follow your dreams and experience life to its fullest. It is called a roadmap for safe traveling.

- There is a curve called failure,
- A loop called confusion,
- Speed bumps called friends,
- Red lights called enemies,
- Caution lights called family,
- You will have flats called jobs, But
- If you have a spare tire called determination,
- An engine called perseverance,
- Insurance called faith, and
- A driver called God,
- You will make it to a place called success.
- This is your roadmap for safe traveling.

Congratulations and God speed as you go forth to be of service.

YOUR COMMITMENT TO THE

PURSUIT OF EDUCATION

I am pleased to accept the invitation of Rachelle and Roy Allen to come and spend time with the junior and senior class this afternoon. If I am not mistaken, I am the only thing standing between you and dismissal so I will be respectful of your time. To use a phrase from the legendary Elizabeth Taylor as she remarked about her eighth husband—"I will not keep you long."

My thanks to your principal—David Hicks—which I have met on other occasions. In my talk I will share some brief moments about my journey in life, however I will share three stories with you that could serve as motivation and inspiration for you.

Diamonds of Hope: The Value of One Person

Buried deep within the earth lie vast deposits of diamonds, the world's most precious gem. Although these stones are tremendously valuable, until they are mined they remain useless. They are just glimmering pebbles hidden beneath the surface. Some day these jewels will be unearthed and the world will marvel at their brilliance.

Just as there is a great storehouse of wealth hidden in the vaults of the earth, so is there tremendous wealth buried deep within the mind and soul of each individual. The wealth may be in the form of intelligence, personality, honor, or a myriad of other abilities and attributes which comprise the spectrum of the human spirit.

As I look at promising individuals like each of you, I conclude that you have broken ground at Ranchview High School and you are being lifted up as treasures to the surface—to sparkle in the sunlight. Just as every diamond offers different possibilities, so does each of you possess vast potential and promise which will distinguish you among the accomplished people of the world.

The education and molding that you are receiving here is similar to the refinement process which all diamonds must undergo. Unlike diamonds, however, your refinement process is never complete. There is no end to the number of facets which may adorn and structure your lives. Your task from this day forward is to utilize your individual talents and abilities so that you may always be a diamond that is being polished.

Let me quickly add that the decision to retain this luster, this shine, is one that must be made by each of you—every day in the years to come. Like diamonds, an educated individual can but increase in value.

One of the world's most famous diamonds is not white, but rather, a radiant blue. This diamond is cherished not only for its size and beauty, but also for the uncanny ability to conduct electricity—to energize those objects with which it comes into contact. The jewel I am speaking of is none other than the Hope Diamond; the only one of its kind in the world. Looking before me now, I see an assembly hall filled with equally unique and powerful blue gems, capable of electrifying the world. I believe that each of you represents a true "diamond of hope."

Tricks of James Lofton

The second story is from the world of sports. I happen to enjoy watching football, basketball, golf and baseball games. I recall seeing an interview with the football great James Lofton, one of the all-time greats of the

Buffalo Bills. The interviewer asked him what tricks he used to be such an outstanding wide receiver. This was Lofton's reply:

"*First trick—work harder than the other guy.*"
"*Second trick—always hustle.*"
"*Third trick—study and know what you are doing.*"
"*Fourth trick—always be prepared.*"
"*Fifth trick—never give up. Those are my tricks.*"
I commend the "tricks" of football star James Lofton to each of you.

The Station

This final story is designed to illustrate what life is all about. Tucked away in our mind is an idyllic vision. We see ourselves on a long trip that spans the continent. We are traveling by train. Out the windows we drink in the passing scene of cars on nearby highways, of children waving at a crossing, of cattle grazing on a distant hillside, of smoke pouring from a power plant, of row upon row of corn and wheat, of flatlands and valleys, of mountains and rolling hillsides, of city skylines and village malls.

But uppermost in our minds is the final destination. We envision that on a certain day at a certain hour we will pull into the station. Bands will be playing and flags waving. Once we get there, we think, so many wonderful dreams will come true and the pieces of our lives will fit together like a completed jigsaw puzzle. So restlessly we pace the aisles; just waiting to arrive at the station.

We say to ourselves, when we reach the station we will be set for life. The puzzle will have been completed. However, sooner or later we must realize that there is no station. There is no one place to arrive at once and for all. The true joy of life is the trip. The station is only a dream. It constantly outdistances us.

So my advice to you students is enjoying life, but never rest on your laurels. Remember the tricks of James Lofton. When I was growing up my father planted this thought in mind, which I commend to you—"If you want to get ahead—get something in your head." Don't ever forget that. Remember my ad libs about my personal journey and the value that I placed on education.

As I leave you, remember this expression that I share with my colleagues. I ask them the question—"what is the largest room in your house?" You answered just as they did the first time. Some of you said the living room, some said the family room. Remember students, the largest room in your house is the "room for improvement."

Thank you for permitting me to share these thoughts with you today. Best wishes and do keep studying, living and working hard.

TAKING OWNERSHIP OF THE OUTCOME

It was my privilege to serve on the founding board of directors for the original Dallas CAN Academy that was founded by Grant East and housed in a trailer on the Buckner property. It was a first of its kind in 1984 and was designed to give boys a second chance.

The experiences were so notable during that early period that there was the expected cry and plea for the program to be expanded to provide an opportunity for girls. A second trailer was obtained. The fantastic journey was now underway.

When I reflect on what has happened since the fateful beginning, I am reminded of a story that I often cite from a book titled <u>Secret Place</u>. The title is "Living Stones." There is a message that those who lead <u>America CAN</u> will find meaning in.

"On the island of Jersey, in the English Channel, stands an old stone church. It has withstood the ravages of time, even though much of the cliff on which it was built has been worn away by the water and storms of the passing centuries.

The walls of the church are made of stones of all sizes, for every member of the congregation contributed to them at least one stone, the best he could carry. The Master Builder used them all. There they are to this day. The rocks brought by the men have their place in the foundation. Stones large and small are there, and even pebbles that mothers had placed in the tiny hands of the babies are there.

That old building stands as a symbol of what a church can be in a community—each worshiper and worker an essential living stone. We are needed, and the Master Builder has a place for each of us. Whoever will may come—enriching the church by becoming an instrument for the grace of God."

Today there are multiple schools in many cities in the Texans CAN program: Dallas, Ft. Worth, Houston, Austin, and San Antonio. Then there are the new schools in St. Louis, Baton Rouge, and Phoenix. It all started with the "rocks" represented by trailers, other buildings, and many people who have made their contributions.

I recall hearing people say that it was impossible to craft a "recovery" educational program that was provided free of charge. I agree that something is impossible until it is accomplished. Let me share a couple of examples to support my assertion.

In 1927, Charles Lindberg flew alone from New York to Paris. He had no radar, no radio, no parachute, and no automatic pilot. He could see nothing out of his front windshield because a spare gas tank had been welded to it.

Lindberg flew for over 33 hours without sleep. He could look forward only by using a periscope that was made from two pocket mirrors.

What Lindberg was impossible until he did it. Something is impossible only until it is accomplished.

The English Channel is 22 miles wide. Its waters are angry and cold. Thousands of athletes have tried to swim the channel most have failed.

In 1961, a 42-year-old man from Argentina swam the English Channel. It too Antonio Albertondo 19 hours to make his swim. When he came ashore in France, his friends congratulated him for accomplishing what they thought was impossible at his age.

He paused for a few minutes to sip a hot drink. Then he told his friends they had not seen the impossible yet, but were about to.

With that, Antonio dove back into the water and swam for 22 more hours; all the way back to England. Impossible? Yes. Accomplished? Yes.

I say again, something is impossible only until it is accomplished.

Mary Fasano's parents pulled her out of the 8th grade so she could work in a cotton mill in Rhode Island. Fifty-five years later, Mary decided to go back to school. She went to high school at night, and at 71 years old, Mary Fasano got her high school diploma. I believe that Mary, Antonio and Charles all took ownership of the outcome.

But I have not finished with the story about Mary Fasano. After receiving her high school diploma she enrolled in Harvard University's extension program and took one course at a time. Mary commuted twenty miles to Cambridge every week, every semester; every year; for seventeen years! Mary Fasano graduated from Harvard University at the age of eighty-nine.

Impossible? Perhaps. Accomplished? Yes. I believe that Mary Fasano took ownership of the outcome in her life.

Those of you who are associated with this unique program that provides opportunity are all stars and you all have more; more to give, more to do, and more to be.

The pioneers of this program never settled for mediocrity—or even success—they settled only for excellence.

That has been the key element supporting this program over the years. You have caused the students to embrace excellence. They have been taught that the pursuit of excellence is never easy, and that it requires confidence, persistence, and perspective.

> *They have been taught that in order to take ownership of the outcome they had to . . .*
> *Believe in themselves—that is confidence.*
> *They must never give in—that is persistence.*
> *They must always be positive—that is perspective.*

Just a couple more stories and I will be through.

A visitor to one of Henry Ford's auto plants met Mr. Ford after a tour of the factory. The visitor was in awe of what he had seen. "It seems impossible," the visitor told Ford, "that a man who started with nothing could accomplish all this."

Ford replied, "You say that I started with nothing, but you are wrong. I started with all I needed. So does everyone—everyone starts with all they need to do anything." Henry Ford had confidence.

A little nun was on a mission to the Appalachian Mountains. She was in a hurry and drove past the last gas station without noticing that she needed gas. She ran out of gas soon after, and had to walk back to the station. The attendant told her that he would like to help her, but had no container to hold her gas.

Still he did want to help, so the attendant agreed to search through an old shed out back to see if there was something that might suffice. The only container that he could find was an old bedpan. The grateful nun told the attendant that the bedpan would work just fine. She carried the gasoline to her car, taking care not to spill a drop.

When she got to her car. The nun carefully poured the contents of the bedpan into her gas tank. As she was doing that, a truck driver pulled alongside the car.

He rolled down his window, shook his head and said, "Now sister, that is what I call faith!" As you seek to take ownership of the outcome, you need to have faith in yourself, and in the mission of the organization. Have confidence.

And after you have confidence, you need persistence. We all remember the words of Winston Churchill when he said "never give in. Never give in. Never give in. In all things large or small, great or petty; never, never, never, give in."

Churchill knew what he was talking about. It took him 3 years to get through the sixth grade because he had trouble learning English. But he never gave in, and he was not alone.

It took Leonardo Da Vinci 10 years to paint the last supper. One painting; ten years. But he never gave in.

Michelangelo spent six years lying on his back on a scaffold painting the Sistine Chapel. By the time he finished, he was virtually blind from the paint that had dripped into his eyes. But he never gave in.

Then there was a little girl from Tennessee who was born to face poverty, obesity, a broken home and physical abuse. Today, she is a multimillionaire and one of the most recognizable celebrities in the world. Who is she?

That's right. She is Oprah Winfrey. Oprah never gave in. Be like the examples that I have shared with you.

  Emily Dickinson once wrote that:
Hope is a thing with feathers

That perches in the soul
And sings a tune without words
And never stops at all.

As you engage in the task of taking ownership of the outcome (and teach your students to do the same) listen to Emily. Let hope perch on your soul. Never stop singing.

File this final story away and use it with students (or even yourself) as you embrace and teach "taking ownership of the outcome." It's the kind of story that would fit in the "Winner's Circle" if that is still practiced.

Picture me standing in front of you holding up a ten thousand dollar bill between the thumb and forefinger of my right hand. Would you want it? Yes? Good! Now, picture me crumbling that bill in my hand and throwing it on the floor. Would you still want that bill? Yes? Good again! Now, watch me step on the crumbled bill with my foot and grind it into the rug. Would you still want that bill? Yes? Congratulations, you have just passed a test in value. No matter what I did to that ten thousand dollar bill, you still wanted it because it had not lost its value. It would still be worth ten thousand dollars.

Sometimes, we are like that bill. People and events in our lives crumble us up, toss us aside, and even grind us down. But no matter what has happened, or what will happen, we never lose our value. We are always worth more than ten thousand dollar bills.

As we take ownership of the outcome we should remember just how valuable we are.

Keep shining! Nothing is impossible until it is accomplished.

THINGS I WISH I WOULD HAVE KNOWN
ABOUT PREPARING FINANCIALLY FOR COLLEGE

Let me begin by applauding Tim and Tamara Williams for having the foresight to plan for Compass 2010: Your Financial Guide for College. To the parents who are here, you are wise to join your son or daughter as they take in valuable information to assist in the drama of attending and paying for a college or university degree.

To the young people, congratulations on your decision to embark upon a journey that will reap a lifetime of benefits. Speaking as someone who has "been there, done that," I can tell you from experience that even though pursuing higher education requires great sacrifice, I can honestly say that it has all been worth it!

I am the oldest of nine children and I was the first to graduate from college. Even though I am from another era, most of you are somewhat the same way I was; you only have limited knowledge about financial options. In my case I went to the only college that was affordable for me and my parents. As scholarship aid was limited (this was long before the advent of Pell grants, and a wide variety of loan options), I had to actively look for a job on campus. Because I was an outstanding typist, I worked as a student secretary for my entire four-year college experience.

Enough about me. You are going to be exposed to a wealth of helpful information today. Take in all that you can at these important sessions:

- *The admissions process*
- *Financial aid and scholarship sources and options*
- *Saving for college*
- *Banking 101 for Students*

Whether your plans are to attend a local community college (and I can attest to the fact that you have some outstanding ones to choose from), or a four year institution, keep this in mind: THERE IS NO SUCH THING AS FREE LUNCH. Financing your college education is a huge issue and you can't wait until the last minute to start planning for it.

When you walk on that college campus, wherever it may be, your higher learning adventure will include a great education, a variety of experiences, and result in your making lifelong relationships. But all of these wonderful things come at a cost. One of the biggest challenges that you will face as a student is finding answers to your many questions about how to finance your education.

I want to leave you some key points as you prepare for attend these rich breakout sessions:

- ➤ *You have to learn to ask the RIGHT questions so that you don't wander aimlessly through the financing maze.*
- ➤ *You have to be prepared to ask the right questions because you will learn that you do have financial aid options.*
- ➤ *Many prospective students make the mistake of thinking that the only financial aid option is student loans. Your available options include scholarships, work-study grants, Pell grant awards, and finally student loans. Learn the full range of options.*

➢ *Compile a binder dedicated to your FA documents.*

➢ *When learning to finance an education keep in mind that there are some very good options to explore BEFORE taking out that loan. Inquire about options in advance of your need.*

➢ *Search out scholarship availability. The best feature of a scholarship is that it does not have to be paid back. There are specific criteria and a detailed application process, with deadlines. Scholarships do not seek you!*

➢ *You can scope out scholarships before you enroll in college. Here at this church we award a little over $100,000 in scholarships to members of the congregation WHO MEET CERTAIN CRITERIA. The same is probably true of other churches, clubs, social organizations, etc. I belong to a men's social organization and we award ten (10) $1500 scholarships to male students.*

➢ *Get help on how to write the best possible scholarship application letter.*

➢ *Make friends with your financial aid advisor once you enroll in college. Always—ask the right questions.*

➢ *Start early in looking for job opportunities. Become a good bulletin board scout. Many job openings are posted on bulletin boards and websites. There is nothing wrong with working!*

➢ *Keep these points in mind regarding grants:*
  * *You must apply for grants on your FAFSA each year.*
  * *Federal Pell Grants are need-based, so you will need to provide information about family finances.*
  * *Most schools provide additional grants based on need.*
  * *Most students can quality.*
  * *You must be persistent.*
  * *I say again, ASK THE RIGHT QUESTIONS.*

Now I must say a few words about loans—I call these points'
things to remember:

➢ *Taking out a student loan is a major responsibility.*
➢ *Loans are not "free money", they must be paid back.*
➢ *You should exhaust all of your non-loan options before*
   considering student loans.
➢ *Discuss the loan option thoroughly with your FA advisor.*
➢ *ASK THE RIGHT QUESTIONS.*

Now a few parting words. Make today the first day in the best
years of your life to come by getting grounded on the facts, and
the "in's and out'" of becoming financial literate. Take in all
of the break-out sessions; ask the right questions (even if you
think they are dumb questions); get the facts from the college
representatives who are here.

Try very hard to go down the "pay-as-you-go" path rather than
take on unnecessary debt through loans that must be paid back.

The college experience is a once-and-a-lifetime experience.
However it will require hard work and discipline.

GO FOR IT!

THE HURDLES AWAITING THE
NEW GRADUATE

It is always an honor for me to be asked by a colleague and friend to address the graduating class where he is serving as a college/university president. It is an honor to be here at Grambling State University. Whenever I am asked to assume this responsibility, I find myself pleased and also challenged. I am pleased because this is a unique honor. I am challenged for I feel compelled to share a message that has to do with particular hurdles that will confront each member of this class as you build your future lives.

You prepare to leave this institution with the benefit of an outstanding education. You are well versed in your areas of study, and equipped with the skills you will need to build your careers.

You are justifiably proud of your accomplishments. You now have the one ingredient that is absolutely necessary for success in any field—enthusiasm. I can see it in your faces as you await your diploma. Why then do you ask, am I here to speak about hurdles?

The answer is simple. Because they are waiting for you right on the other side of this ceremony. And it is not only important that you clear these hurdles, as I know you will, but that you can clear them in the right way.

Ultimately, that is what will justify the education that you have received at this great university, and will give meaning to your entire life.

Let's consider for a moment what is going on in the broader world that exists outside of this campus. Our nation has won the Cold War—but lost the War on Poverty. We have achieved the ability to impose our national will almost anywhere on the face of the planet—but have shown ourselves completely unwilling to provide a secure and safe environment within our own cities. We have gained the power to enforce our sense of appropriate human rights around the globe. But have found it necessary to put a higher percentage of our citizenry behind bars than any other country, including South Africa during the darkest days of apartheid.

We are the richest nation in the world, but we say we cannot afford to provide lunches to our school children. We have more billionaires and millionaires than at any other time in our nation's history, and yet we have more children growing up in poverty than ever before. We have achieved a level of material comfort that has never been rivaled; and yet we have seen hundreds of thousands of young people attempt to escape that reality through the self-destructive venue of illicit drugs.

We have seen some of our churches falter, and many of our families fall apart. Yet we see youth gangs proliferate in virtually every community of our nation. We have seen firearms become as common as bicycles, while the expected life span of young African-American males continues to decline. We have seen our society become more polarized than every before, while a ground swell of public opinion tells us that the day of affirmative action has passed. And we have seen millions of families lose their middle class status to economic dislocation, while more and more people want to reform our welfare system out of existence.

Please do not misunderstand me. My comments have nothing to do with political parties. They are not meant to condemn or endorse anyone or anything. I am simply referencing issues for you to consider that cut much deeper than political parties, and they touch each and every one of us.

For we live at a time in which it is all too easy to focus on ourselves, and forget the larger picture. We live at a time in which it is easy to lose sight of our hopes and responsibilities; because it can be so very difficult simply to meet our personal needs and ambitions. We live at a time in which there may well be legitimate reasons to keep our heads down. To forget our idealism, or at least to put it away for another day. In short, we live at a time in which much of the spirit that built institutions like this one, and which has been passed on to each of you graduates, may seem to be old-fashioned and out of step.

Let me assure you, members of this graduating class that is definitely not the case. Far from being an encumbrance, the sense of purpose that you have gained here is an absolute necessity if you intend to live your life with self-respect and compassion. While others look to their own welfare, you have the ability to help provide for the welfare of others. While most young men and women seek personal security or wealth, you have the ability to work for the advancement of a broader group. While a majority of your peers accept the values of today as the only guideposts to success, you can draw on a deeper and far richer tradition to add meaning to your lives, and value to the communities in which you live.

What am I asking you to do? I am not asking you to life a life of selfless service, although some of you may choose to do that. I am not asking you to deny yourself the benefits of advancement in your chosen career. I am not asking you to take a vow of poverty.

But I am asking you to recognize that dollars and cents are just one measure of an individual's worth, and not a very reliable one at that. Rather, the true test is what the individual does for their community and for mankind.

You can make your contribution to the board room, or the classroom, or the court room. You can help make the world a better place as an engineer; as a health care professional; an artist; or in any other of a wide range of fields. But in making the world a better place, you are also making a better life for yourself. In making the world a better place, you are also making yourself a better person. And that is one lesson you must never forget, if you are to be true to the idealism that has characterized this venerable institution of higher education throughout its history.

A second lesson that I urge you to keep in mind as you leave Grambling State University has to do with one of the sinister aspects of the society in which we live. While progress has been made, and while attitudes of many Americans have changed over the past several decades, we would be naïve to ignore the fact that racism is very much alive in America.

Each of you, and I can guarantee it, will confront racism in some form during your careers. On this matter I am speaking from experience. It will probably be subtle. It will bear little resemblance to the overt and often violent forms that racism took not all that many years ago. But it will be racism just the same. While racism will always be a burden, you must never let it be an excuse. While racism will always be unacceptable in others, you cannot permit racism to limit your aspirations and achievements. We must take the world as we find it if we are to have any hope of providing for our own security, and improving the lot of others. As discouraging as the attitudes, remarks and actions that you will experience, you will be primary losers if they prevent you from achieving your goals. Your life will be lessened;

your aspirations will be unfulfilled; your living standards will stagnate; and worst of all, your ability to contribute will go unrecognized.

But if I must be honest in warning you of the subtle racism that will confront you as you leave this university, I can also be optimistic about other factors that are active in our world. More and more corporations and institutions are demonstrating that they value diversity and are open to new attitudes and values. My prediction is that the days of racism are numbered, and that narrow-minded bigotry cannot long survive at any company that intends to compete within our diverse society.

And if racism cannot survive in the work place, it cannot survive anywhere in America over the long run. So, as you confront racism during your work life, it will be a burden, but only a temporary burden, and one that you will be increasingly able to bear. Why? Because of the preparation that you have received as a student at this university.

The third lesson that I would leave with you today is drawn from my personal experience. But I predict that it will have applicability to many, if not all of the graduates who are here today.

It is simply this. As you move through your lives, you cannot be in the process of getting ready when opportunity comes your way. You must actually be ready when opportunity comes your way. You must have already equipped yourself with the skills and attitudes you need to achieve your objective. For a goal, without the skills needed to achieve that goal, is nothing. In fact, it is worse than nothing. It is simply wishful thinking that can divert you from your real work.

I started out my career with the intention of becoming a chief business officer or a college or university. Desirably this would become my lot at a historically black college or university. It took me almost eighteen years to realize that objective. However, I recall very vividly the president who hired me as a vice president at Morgan State University, telling me that I had prepared myself well for the challenge of being a chief financial and business officer. And, as a result, beat out a number of individuals with broader titles and higher places in their respective organizations.

I was ready when the opportunity presented itself. And I urge you to be ready as well, when whatever objective you have set for yourself comes looking for you. I have a theory about life and that theory is that the more prepared you are, the more opportunities you will be offered. In fact, you'll get opportunities that were meant for others simply because they were not ready.

Such was the case when I became a college president for the first time. Being a college president had not been a goal of mine, but others thought hat I had the capabilities and attributes. And so, a college business officer was able to move to the pinnacle of his profession simply by being ready when the opportunity presented itself.

For the workplace of today, and even more the workplace of tomorrow, will offer incredible breadth of opportunities. Dare to set your goals high, because given the pace of change that is currently occurring, almost every goal can be realized—if you are ready. The members of this graduating class will compete in a global marketplace. You will deal with ideas that have originated in other cultures. You will work with technologies that are only beginning to originate within the imagination of men and women around the world.

As you leave this institution, I urge you to welcome all the opportunities that life gives you to grow and develop. While today may mark the end of your formal instruction at this point in time, it should not mark the end of either your ability, or your desire to learn. For when it is all said and done, the most valuable gift that any institution of higher learning can provide is not to be found in a textbook or a course syllabus. It is to be seen in the habits of curiosity and hard work that characterizes its graduates. It reveals itself in their desire to continue learning, and in their willingness to view education as a lifelong commitment.

Each of you will face many hurdles as you build your future. And you will not make it over each with equal success. But you will succeed if you maintain the high sense of purpose and idealism that characterize Grambling State University. You will succeed if you recognize that despite the vestiges of racism that still plaque society, your contributions are crucial. You will succeed if you are ready to act when opportunity comes your way. And you will succeed if you sustain your curiosity and your ability to learn throughout your entire life.

Ladies and gentlemen, graduates, I know that I add my wishes of success to those of your families and to those fine educators and leaders at this university. Even more important, however, I know that you are well equipped to make those wishes mesh into reality. And in that, you have my sincere congratulations, and my respect, as you set forth to rebuild our world.

Godspeed one and all.

THE TOOLS AND QUALITIES OF
EFFECTIVE LEADERSHIP

I am truly privileged to have been asked to deliver the commencement addresses at both the morning and afternoon services at Dallas Baptist University this year. I consider this a unique honor and privilege.

President Cook, trustees, faculty and administration, support staff, guests and the members of the graduating class—greetings to all you and congratulations to the graduates.

In view of the mission commitment to servant leadership, my remarks will be framed around the subject of leadership.

In spite of all the imperfections in the world and our daily hassles, the state of our species is good, and is much better than it has ever been. You live a life that Roman emperors could not even dream of. Even the most battered of our motor cars travel faster than the fastest Roman chariot. We can get a light at the lip of a switch and King Henry VIII never had that.

In 150 years we have gone from the Pony Express to the telegraph; to the telephone; to the cell phone; to the Internet; and to the wireless Web.

The progress of our species over the last 150 years has been phenomenal and that progress accelerates. I am confident that your generation, and the generations to follow, will live better, longer and hopefully, more fulfilling lives than any previous generation. All of this, however, is predicated upon your capacity to deal with that which is required of our leaders.

I believe that you have been taught here that leadership requires three essential characteristics: available, accountable, and vulnerable. You have also been taught here that there are two tools, among others, that every leader needs. Those tools being writing skills and speaking skills.

But I believe that you have also been taught that there is one quality without which no leader will last, and that quality is character. What is character? Your character is what you are when no one is looking. In short it is what you are and do in secret.

Let me add a final element in the toolbox of the future leader, and that is excellence. Some have been exposed to the book <u>Good to Great</u> by Jin Collins. The author's thesis is that if anyone settles for just being good, you will in time begin to retrogress and decline. Therefore, you should always strive to be great— which translates into the pursuit of excellence.

Excellence is something that we are always reaching for. It is akin to an expression that I use with some regularity with my colleagues and students. "The largest room in any house is the room for improvement."

You have tasted excellence here at Dallas Baptist University. Pursue excellence over and over, incessantly. There are three things that excellence requires—confidence, persistence, and perspective.

A few brief words about each of those elements and I will be through and you can begin the process of receiving your diplomas.

To excel you must never give in. That is persistence. And to excel, you must always be positive. That is perspective.

A visitor in one of Henry Ford's auto plants met Ford after a tour of the factory. The visitor was in awe of what he had seen. He said to Mr. Ford, "It seems impossible that a man who started with nothing could accomplish all of this."

Ford replied, "You say that I started with nothing, but you are wrong. I started with all that I needed. So does everyone start with all they need to do anything."
Reflecting on the words of Ford, as you leave here, remember that you have all you need to do anything. That's called confidence.

After you have confidence, have persistence. Winston Churchill said to the people of Great Britain in the darkest days of World War II—"Never give in. Never give in. In all things large or small, great or petty, never, never, never give in."

Churchill was speaking from experience for it took him three years to get through the sixth grade because he had trouble learning English. But Churchill never gave in.

Michelangelo spent six years lying on his back on a scaffold painting the Sistine Chapel. By the time he finished, he was virtually blind from the paint that had dripped into his eyes. But he never gave in.

Perhaps everyone here can remember the children's book— Green Eggs and Ham—written by Dr. Seuss. The first of his many books was rejected by twenty-three publishers before a little known firm accepted his work. He never gave in.

Be like Churchill. Be like Michelangelo. Be like Dr. Seuss. Never give in. Have boundless persistence.

Emily Dickinson once wrote these words that relate to the quality of persistence. "Hope is a thing with feathers that perches in the soul and sings a tune without words, and never stops at all." Listen to Emily. Let hope perch on your soul. Never let it stop singing. Never give in. Have persistence.

Perspective is how we look at things. And there is a positive and a negative way to look at everything. If you want to continue achieving excellence, always be positive. Find happiness in all that you do.

Don't be so focused on the details, challenges and burdens of your life that you never notice its beauty—its fragrance and its flowers. Every success that you enjoy is a flower that will blossom and grow. Its petals will open. And each petal will have a different kind of beauty. Each success will have its own kind of beauty—and you will give birth to that beauty.

Dallas Baptist University is committed to shaping servant leaders. The essential elements that I have stated in this talk have been addressed by many, if not all, of the professors that you have interfaced with. Take those lessons with you as you graduate.

Keep in mind that those who would lead in any walk of life should write their own stories in lives of service to their followers. Let those who would search for the nature of leadership look for evidence of such in significant service. The more significant the service, the more likely the source will be rooted in humility. The simpler the source, the greater the leadership. Humility will get you off to a great start on the path of leadership and, if you prove to be a successful leader, humility will be there to greet you at the end of a satisfying and productive career.

In keeping with the lessons on servant leadership that you have learned here, and as this is a commencement worship service; I want to take must a moment to life up a lesson from the Scriptures.

In the first sermon recorded in his gospel, Matthew spotlights Jesus' major emphasis on values. Jesus knew His first task was to provide a set of core for His disciples. I draw your attention to Jesus' list of values from that sermon.

> ➤ *Do the right thing for the right reasons.*
> ➤ *Pray God's agenda, not your own.*
> ➤ *Relationships will make or break you.*
> ➤ *Prioritize eternal things, not temporal things.*
> ➤ *Don't sweat the small stuff.*
> ➤ *God's kingdom is paramount; seek it first.*
> ➤ *Judge yourself before you judge others.*
> ➤ *If you need something, ask; if you have something, give it.*
> ➤ *Stay true to your convictions; don't wander from the narrow path.*
> ➤ *Obedience to God is the only sure foundation for life.*

Congratulations! Never stop giving! Never stop serving! Lead God's way!

God bless you!

YOUR COMMITMENT TO THE

PURSUIT OF EXCELLENCE

Congratulations to each of the scholars who are being recognized today by the Alpha Epsilon Boule. Commendations also to the parents and family members, who have supported, sustained and guided you. In my talk I will share some brief moments about my journey in life; however I will share three stories with you that could serve as motivation and inspiration for you.

Diamonds of Hope: the Value One Person

Buried deep within the earth lie vast deposits of diamonds, the world's most precious gem. Although these stones are tremendously valuable, until they are mined they remain useless. They are just glimmering pebbles hidden beneath the top soil. Some day these jewels will be unearthed and the world will marvel at their brilliance.

Just as there is a great storehouse of wealth hidden in the vaults of the earth, so is there tremendous wealth buried deep within the mind and soul of each individual. The wealth may be in the form of intelligence, personality, honor, or a myriad of other abilities and attributes which comprise the spectrum of the human spirit.

As I look at promising individuals like each of you, I conclude that you have broken ground in your high school experience, and you are being lifted up as treasures to the surface—to sparkle in the sunlight. Just as every diamond offers different possibilities, so does each of you possess vast potential and promise which will distinguish you among the accomplished people of the world.

The education and molding that you are receiving here is similar to the refinement process through which all diamonds must undergo. Unlike diamonds, however, your refinement process is never complete. There is no end to the number of facets which may adorn and structure your lies. Your task from this day forward is to utilize your individual talents and abilities so that you may always be a diamond that is being polished.

Let me quickly add that the decision to retain this luster, this shine, is one that must be made by each of you—every day in the years to come. Like diamonds, an educated individual can but increase in value.

One of the world's most famous diamonds is not white, but rather it is a radiant blue. This diamond is cherished not only for its size and beauty, but also for the uncanny ability to conduct electricity—to energize those objects with which it comes into contact. The jewel I am speaking of is none other than the Hope Diamond; the only one of its kind in the world. Looking before me now, I see an assembly hall filled with equally unique and powerful blue gems; all capable of electrifying the world. I believe that each one of you represents a true "diamond of hope."

Tricks of James Lofton

The second story is from the world of sports. I happen to enjoy watching football, basketball, golf, tennis, and baseball games. I recall seeing an interview with the football great James Lofton, one of the all=time greats of professional football. The interviewer asked him what tricks he used to be such an outstanding wide receiver. This was Lofton's reply.

"First trick—work harder than the other guy."
"Second trick—always hustle."
"Third trick—study and know what you are doing."
"Fourth trick—always be prepared."
"Fifth trick—never give up." Those are my tricks.

I commend the "tricks" of football star James Lofton to each of you.

The Station

This final story is designed to illustrate what life is all about. Tucked away in our mind is an idyllic vision. We see ourselves on a long trip that spans the continent. We are traveling by train. Out the windows we drink in the passing scene of cars on nearby highways; of children waving at a crossing; of cattle grazing on a distant hillside; of smoke pouring from a power plant; of row upon row of core and wheat; of flatlands and valleys; of mountains and rolling hillsides; of city skylines and village malls.

But uppermost in our minds is the final destination. We envision that on a certain day at a certain hour we will pull into the station. Bands will be playing and flags waving. Once we get there, we think, so many wonderful dreams will come true and the pieces of our lives will fit together like a completed jigsaw puzzle. So restlessly we pace the aisles; just waiting to arrive at the station.

We say to ourselves, when we reach the station we will be set for life. The puzzle will have been completed. However, sooner or later we must realize that there is no station. There is no one place to arrive at once and for all. The true joy of life is the trip. The station is only a dream. It constantly outdistances us.

So my advice to you students is to enjoy life, but never rest on your laurels. Remember the tricks of James Lofton. When I was growing up my father planted this thought in my mind, which I commend to you. He said, "Junior, if you want to get ahead, get something in your head." Don't every forget that.

As I leave you, remember this expression that I share with my colleagues. I ask them the question—"What is the largest room in your house?" I ask you that question. You answered just as they did the first time. Some of you said the living room; said the family room. Remember graduates, the largest room in your house is the "room for improvement."

As some of you will be pursuing careers in the arena of health and medicine, this little tidbit from the experience and practice of Dr Louis Pasteur has significance. He would tell his medical students at the end of each class, "Young men as you go through life, always take your life preserver with you. Your life preserver is curiosity." Stay curious young men.

Thank you for permitting me to share these thoughts with you today. Best wishes and do keep studying, living and working hard.

GRADUATION AND LIFE

My objective in this talk tonight as I address four graduating classes in the Carrollton/farmers Branch Independent School District is to impress upon you what the meaning of graduation is, and to motivate you to continue on your quest for success and achievement.

The word "graduation" has several meanings. The primary meaning is the state of being arranged in steps or degrees. Tonight you are graduating from one phase of life to another, because life is a series of progressions.

Life is like a day. There are the early morning hours of babyhood; the morning of youth; the high noon of maturity; and then evening. Each of you now moves from morning toward noon.

But what else is life? Life is measured in deed, not just the passing of time; not merely money-making; nor is life just fame or brilliance. When one reaches the point where you are tonight, you have accomplished an important goal. But there are a number of things that should also happen to you as you reach the time of "graduation."

You should see in clearer perspective the great moral principles of live. The things of worth should really stand out now. You should be able to recall the past and dream of what lies ahead for you. You should be able to take both a backward look and a look beyond. The backward look is important for you can now examine what has been achieved as you reached this point in your lives. You can ponder those things that have been most important. At graduation one can see life as continuous and now you should begin pondering that which lies ahead for you . . .

Remember that life is a gift so don't squander it. Don't waste it. Don't let it slip away. Be grateful for this precious gift of life and spend it by being as happy, thankful, and useful as you possibly can.

Let gratitude be your attitude as you move to the next phase of your life. Our lives are marvelous for life is a priceless treasure. It is more valuable than anything else in this world. It is to be guarded with the utmost care, and to be used for the noblest purposes.

What is life? I'm glad you are joining with me as I continue to craft an answer to that question. Ponder this illustration. Life is like a spring, a brook, a river, an ocean, and a vapor. Like rain, it is a cycle that is continuous.

Every time that you graduate, and I am hopeful that this will not be your last graduation. Higher education lies in front of you, plus you are going into a bigger world
Where there are more people to know; more difficult jobs to do; more experiences to have than you have yet to encounter.

One of the things which graduation says is that you are now ready to get more out of life. Your high school experiences should have awakened you to the world of possibilities.

The graduation ceremony and the diploma that you will receive tell the world that you are now ready to go ahead to the next step in your lives. You have passed through an important part of the learning process. If this experience has been successful, it should also have taught you that there is much more to learn.

It is important for you to always believe in yourself and to comprehend that you can do more than you have already done. This is not the time to rest on your laurels. You must keep in front of you that no matter how much you have done, you can and must do more.

Never settle for just being average or mediocre. Strive always for excellence. Pursue excellence continually. Excellence takes confidence, persistence, and it takes perspective. Keep at it! Never give in!

As you shine and strive for excellence, keep this illustration in focus. Picture me standing in front of you holding up a ten thousand dollar bill, between the thumb and forefinger of my right hand. Tell me, would you want it? Yes? Now, picture me crumbling that bill in my hand and throwing it on the floor. Would you still want it? Yes? Good again.

Now watch me step on the crumbled bill with my foot and grind it on the floor would you still want the bill? Yes? Well, congratulations, you have just passed a test in value. No matter what I did to that ten thousand dollar bill, you still wanted it, because it had not lost its value. It would still be worth ten thousand dollars.

Sometimes, we like the bill. People and events in our lives crumble us up, toss us aside, and even grind us down. But no matter what has happened, or what will happen, we never lose our value. We are always worth more than ten thousand dollar bills.

Remember that little story. Remember that you are valuable. You have climbed up the mountain at your respective high schools. It was easier for some of you than for others. But for all of you, it is an accomplishment which must be applauded. So, we congratulate you. Best wishes for your future.

BE TRUE TO YOURSELF

I am pleased to address the recipients of graduate degrees at Texas A&M University. To celebrate your accomplishments and especially that treasured doctoral hood which the doctoral degree recipient will soon adorn is a special moment. I am sure that all of us who have gone through this experience will tell you that the treasured diploma will be one of your passports for life.

Certainly the degree to be conferred on you today is a milestone. It opens up a new world of possibilities for you. With your advanced education you will find that anything is possible. With that in mind, let me suggest that today is also a day to honor and remember your first teachers—your parents and family members. My parents and early teachers equipped me with principles that have served me well throughout my life and my career.

Because of my upbringing, I have become a very task-oriented person. The principles that were instilled in me and taught me, have served me well. Permit me to share just a few with you in this short address.

The first principle is—"Stand up and be counted." Graduates, you have a new set of tools at your disposal. These tools for critical and creative thinking and research allow you to challenge the process and to question the status quo. You will be called on to do just that from this day forward.

The second principle is—"Lead with your heart, and not just your head." Many of you are already in the business and professional world, and you are used to thinking your way through issues and challenges. I will be first to say, never stop thinking and keep at it!

But how about the "feeling" part—your heart! We need your contribution of heart and soul, your compassion, both in your arena of work, and in the larger community. In these times in which we live, compassion is critical and it comes from the heart.

The third principle is—"Endeavor to make a difference each and every day." This is especially true if we embrace this as a personal responsibility and act upon it each day.

Consider Marian Wright Edelman, who founded the Children's Defense Fund, which is today the most powerful lobby for children. She said, "We must not, in trying to think about how we can make a difference, ignore the small daily differences we can make, which, over time, add to big differences we often cannot foresee."

This may be at home, at work, in our children's schools, in places of worship, and elsewhere in the community. Whatever the arena may be, the rewards are in knowing you have helped as you reached beyond self. You may say, this altruism sounds great, but are there rewards? Just what are those rewards, at least in terms of one's career?

I am here to say that the rewards of those forms of serving, far outweigh any sacrifices and, in fact, do come back many-fold in life.

Looking back on my own career, I am particularly mindful of the memories when I received my doctoral degree. I figured that the degree would be my ticket to additional career advancement, maybe even becoming a CFO or CEO someday.

A mentor, however, stopped me cold in my tracks after he had congratulated me. He told me that the degree alone would not be the major determinant of success in my career. It would certainly help, for one year later I did become a chief financial officer of a university. He also reminded me of advice given him early in his career, when he was told—"The more you give, the more you get back—it is an unending cycle." I can testify to the truth of that bit of sage advice.

Giving back to others is a fundamental principle that carries us ahead. As we give back to others we get so much back. We learn about others. We learn about ourselves, and we learn how best to inspire and lead others.

Does it work? To make a long story short, I have received numerous promotions in higher education and in community service. I have received presidential appointments; appointments to corporate boards; and other major venues for service. But those accolades and opportunities came my way only after heeding that wise advice of my mentor.

My promotions, appointments, and my current job as the chancellor of one of the largest community college systems in the nation, have all come as a result of my expertise, but also came as a result of my volunteer work in the community.

Another benefit is intangible. There is powerful emotional satisfaction from seeing individual lives changed for the better as a result of your efforts, even small efforts, to make a difference.

Sometimes in life I reflect that it is better to be lucky rather than good. I have been both, thanks indeed to my education, for which I am forever grateful, and thankful for the wise counsel that I was given.

Let me re-emphasize that becoming involved in the community is a wise thing to do. In my experience, the social fabric of the community is intricately intertwined with success in business, education, and in the professions. And more especially, the social fabric of the community is intertwined with becoming a successful person. The two are one.

So today we celebrate your hard-earned success. Along with friends, family, and the dedicated faculty and staff of this university, let me say congratulations on this day of joy and accomplishment.

For tomorrow and the rest of your life, I wish you well. You have been molded and shaped, and are now prepared to move to the next phase of your lives. You are well-prepared! Go forth and service as well! Make this university proud of you always. Congratulations and now the time for the long awaited hood!

PART TWO

EDUCATION STARTS, NOT ENDS
WITH THE DIPLOMA

Selected Quotations

EDUCATION STARTS, NOT ENDS,
WITH THE DIPLOMA

"You can make a difference in the world by developing your own character. I want you to feel and become human beings. You've got to respect everybody. Be proud of yourself no matter what you do. College does not teach character. You teach yourself character. And you only learn by recognizing and executing integrity. And in doing that, you're going to change the world."

- **Bill Cosby (Rensselaer Polytechnic Institute)**

"It may seem a heavy burden to be placed on one generation by a member of another. For it's a responsibility, in fact, we share, not to save the world but simply to love it. Meaning—don't hurt it. It's already beaten, scoured, gasping for breath. Don't hurt it. Don't enable others who do and who will."

- **Toni Morrison (Smith College)**

"Insensitivity and intolerance awaits you. Stand up for what is right and speak out against what is wrong. Jim Crow Sr. is dead, but Jim Crow Jr. is alive and well. Don't ever stop in the education process. Remember, what's important is not where you came from, but where you are headed and where you end up ... Don't be afraid to take risks and don't be afraid of failure."

- **Kweisi Mfume (Hampton University)**

""Within you, you have the power to accomplish not only your dreams, but a better tomorrow for all people. The only limitation to your reach is your vision. Set high goals for yourself."

- **Judge Roger L. Gregory (Piedmont Virginia CC)**

"The more you do, the more you get. You're not going to hit the lotto. Quit playing the numbers. Your chances of winning are one in several million and you probably ain't the one. It's your dream and vision that makes you what you are. It ain't got nothing to do with that piece of paper they're going to give you."

- **Steve Harvey (Southern University)**

"You can't choose the world you live in, but you can choose your response to it. You are responsible for your own feelings. Growing up means meeting every challenge with a plan, not wallowing in the pain. Don't be afraid to ask for help, but don't blame others for problems you can solve."

- **U.S. Secretary of Education Rod Paige (Jackson State University)**

"Leading means changing the very definition of success itself. (These non-traditional) graduates are often the ones who mentor young people, who give back to the community and then become community leaders. (They are the ones) who help us redefine what it means to succeed. They lead, not just succeed."

- **Lani Guinier—Professor of Law/Harvard (The University of the District of Columbia)**

"Critical thinking is the very thing missing in our society. Be a critical thinker. Don't allow anyone to tell you what to think. Life is really an open canvas very much like the sky and your gifts and

talents are to be utilized to create the exquisite painting. Our challenge is to use our gifts and our talents and education . . . as a weapon to fight for the rights of people."

- **Susan Taylor—Publication Director/ESSENCE (Dillard University)**

"Don't make a mistake about what is happening here today. The fact that you are about to get a diploma from one of America's finest institutions of higher learning does not mean you are educated. Some of the dumbest people I know have degrees from some of America's finest institutions of higher learning. They took diploma in hot little hand, pronounced themselves educated and proceeded to never read another book, entertain another fresh or new idea and, most tragically for their society and country, never again pay attention to much of anything other than themselves, to much of anything that was happening around them or to others. Please, please, do not to do that."

- **Jim Lehrer—Newshour with Jim Lehrer (Tufts University)**

"There's a big difference between having a career and having a life. Be sure not to confuse the two. At the end of your life, you will never regret not having passed one more test, not winning one more verdict, or closing one more deal. You will regret time not spent with a husband, a friend or a parent."

- **Barbara Bush (Wake Forest University)**

"You don't ever have to do anything sensational in order to love or to be loved. The real drama of life—that which matters most—is rarely center stage or in the spotlight. In fact, it has nothing to do with IQ's and honors and the fancy outsides of life. What really nourishes our souls is knowing that we can be

trusted, that we never have to fear the truth, that the foundation of our very being is good stuff."

- *Fred Rogers—Mister Roger's Neighborhood
  (Marquette University)*

"Many of you will miss success because it comes dressed in overalls and looks like work. What you do for yourselves, you will take to the graveyard. What you do for others will live on in perpetuity."

- *Joe Clark—former Principal of Eastside High School—Paterson, New Jersey
  (Livingston College—Rutgers University)*

"Life will serve up staggering challenges as you go through it. You will find comfort and distress in the most unlikely places. In the eyes of a loved one, in the unexpected death of a good friend, you will find faith. The sheer beauty of the world around you and the laughter of a really good joke will sustain you. What you most need in life will be given to you. In the face of unimaginable anguish there will be joy. I tell you this because I know it to be so. Take heart in that—and have faith."

- *Kelsey Grammer—star of Frasier
  (University of Massachusetts—Amherst)*

"At this moment that I speak, a bomb is tearing apart somebody's father . . . a woman is being raped . . . another woman's throat is being slit because she has dishonored her family in getting pregnant . . . the heart of a young man with AIDS has stopped beating . . . Someone is bribing an official so a stream can be polluted, so drugs can poison a street, so guns can cross a frontier, so justice can be undone.

... Though you did not make the world as it is ... this world now belongs to you ... I have brought up the infinite pain of the world at your graduation because from this solemn and joyous moment onward, you will be faced every day with the decision of whether to rise up against that pain or whether to stand by the wayside and let it continue ... The world does not have to be the way it is ... You can make a difference."

- *Ariel Dorfman—Latin American writer and Duke University Professor*
  (American University)

PART THREE

END NOTES

CONCLUDING EXPRESSIONS

This book contains approximately one-third of the commencement addresses that I have been favored to deliver during my career in higher education. While each message was directed to a specific audience, the reader will note that certain themes are repeated. It is my hope that the reader will be able to discern the importance that I placed on certain thoughts and themes.

My desire and hope is that this collection of messages will prove useful to students, parents, counselors, pastors, mentors, coaches, and educators.

The 21st century is a period of unheard of change and challenges. The words of Louis Pasteur have lasting utility—"Life and all that it entails always favors the prepared mind. As you go through life, be sure to take your life preserver with you—your life preserver is curiosity."

My concluding expression is—"education starts, not ends, with the diploma.

AUTHOR'S BIOGRAPHY

The author began his career in higher education when he was appointed as an Instructor of Business at Alcorn State University immediately upon his graduation from that college. He received specialized training to prepare him for a career as a college/university business officer. His career began at Tuskegee University in Alabama where he served with distinction for seventeen years.

During his tenure there he earned an MBA at Indiana University and the doctorate in higher education administration and finance at Auburn University. He has subsequently engaged in further advanced study at the University of Michigan, Princeton University, and Harvard University, St. Mary's Seminary, and most recently he participated in the Oxford Round Table at Oxford University.

He holds degrees from Alcorn State University, Indiana University and Auburn University. He holds two theological degrees and was awarded the honorary doctor of humanities degree from Dallas Baptist University.

Following his service at Tuskegee University he served as the Vice President for Finance and Management at Morgan State University (Maryland), President of Schenectady County Community College (New York), President of Bishop College in Dallas, and he has served as the President of El Centro College in Dallas for twenty years.

He is a retired Lieutenant Colonel in the U.S. Army Reserve Medical Services Corps. He is an ordained Baptist minister has served as an associate pastor in New York, Mississippi, and Dallas, Texas. He served as the interim pastor of the St. John Missionary Baptist Church in Dallas for a period of approximately three years, and is currently the Associate Pastor for Development for the Concord Baptist Church in Dallas.

He has a long period of service as a teacher and preacher. He served on the faculty of the Congress of Christian Education for the Empire State Baptist Convention in New York, and on the faculty of the Northwest District Association of Christian Education, and the Baptist Missionary and Education Convention of Texas' State Congress of Christian Education. He is a Certified Dean by the National Baptist Convention, U.S.A., Inc.

He served as the Associate Minister for Christian Education and assistant to the Senior Pastor at the historic St. John Missionary Baptist Church of Dallas under the late Dr. Manuel L. Scott, Sr. for a period of twelve years.

As the Associate Pastor for Development for the Concord Missionary Baptist Church he supports the Senior Pastor and staff in the development of economic and public service initiatives for the church.

He has a distinguished record of public service and his areas of interest include education, religion, human services and business.

He has served on the graduate faculty of Dallas Baptist University since 1987 and holds the rank of Distinguished Adjunct Professor. In 2003 he was selected as the John W. Turner

<u>*Outstanding Adjunct Faculty Member*</u> *for the College of Business at the university.*

He has received numerous awards for his service in education, religion, and public service. Notable among the awards is the awarding of the honorary doctor of humanities degree from Dallas Baptist University and election to the Alumni Hall of Honor of the Indiana University Graduate School of Business. He has held two presidential appointments and presently serves on the Board of Directors of the National Endowment for the Humanities, following his nomination by the President and confirmation by the U.S. Senate.

He is a nationally recognized public speaker and is a Distinguished Toastmaster. He has published sermons, speeches, monographs, in-service training manuals, and has a wide library of sermon tapes. He has preached, lectured, and taught in more than thirty states and internationally. He is the author of ten published books and eight monographs of sermons and Christian education training study guides.

In July 2005 he was one of forty-three international educators invited to participate in the <u>Oxford Round Table</u> at the historic Oxford University in England.

In May 2006 after having served as President of El Centro College for twenty years, he was appointed as Chancellor of the seven-college Dallas County Community College District. As the sixth chancellor, he is the first African-American Chancellor of the largest community college in Texas, enrolling over 100,000 students each academic term.

In 2011 he was the recipient of the Russell Perry Servant Leadership Award from Dallas Baptist University, the highest award in Dallas for a servant leader. He was the first African American recipient of that distinguished award.

He and his wife have been married for fifty-two years and they are the parents of a daughter and son, and have two granddaughters. Their daughter is an assistant vice president with J.P. Morgan Chase Bank in Dallas and their son is the chief executive officer of the Alameda County Hospital District in Oakland, California.